THE TIME PARADOX

SUSAN L WILLIAMS

THE TIME PARADOX

About the Author

Dr Susan L Williams DQC BMsc Cl-Hyp is a clinical hypnotherapist, quantum counsellor, and metaphysical researcher committed to helping others reconnect with their innate wisdom and timeless nature.

With a background in mind-body science, consciousness studies, and energy work, Dr. Williams draws on over twenty years of experience guiding individuals toward lives aligned with purpose, regeneration, and inner coherence. Her work challenges cultural assumptions about aging and limitation, inviting clients to return to the natural rhythm of the soul.

Her approach integrates subtle body mapping, hypnotherapy, spiritual psychology, and quantum principles - all grounded in a lived understanding that time is not something to outrun or resist, but something we can engage with consciously and creatively.

Through private sessions, teaching, and writing, Sue has supported countless clients in moving from a sense of urgency or depletion to a deeper connection with who they truly are. Her work invites a shift from managing time to mastering presence - from fragmentation to wholeness.

When she's not working with clients or writing, you'll often find her walking in nature, meditating, or spending quiet time with animals - especially horses, who continually teach her about timing, stillness, and truth.

To learn more, explore offerings, or inquire about sessions:

- Website: https://Holistic-Health.au
- Email: sue@holistic-health.au

Copyright Notice

No part of this book may be reproduced in any form or by any electronic or mechanical means including information storage and retrieval systems, without permission in writing from the author. The only exception is by a reviewer, who may quote short excerpts in a review.

Although the author and publisher have made every effort to ensure that the information in this book was correct at press time, the author and publisher do not assume and hereby disclaim any liability to any party for any loss, damage, or disruption caused by errors or omissions, whether such errors or omissions result from negligence, accident, or any other cause.

This publication is designed to provide accurate and authoritative information with regard to the subject matter covered. It is sold with the understanding that the publisher is not engaged in rendering professional services. If legal advice or other expert assistance is required, the services of a competent professional should be sought.

The fact that an organization or website is referred to in this work as a citation and/or a potential source of further information does not mean that the author or the publisher endorses the information the organization or website may provide or recommendations it may make.

Please remember that Internet websites listed in this work may have changed or disappeared between when this work was written and when it is read.

© 2025 Susan L Williams. All rights reserved.

Disclaimer

The information contained in this book is intended for educational and inspirational purposes only. It is not intended to diagnose, treat, cure, or prevent any medical or psychological condition, nor is it a substitute for professional medical advice, diagnosis, or treatment.

Readers are encouraged to consult a qualified health practitioner before making any changes to their physical, emotional, or mental healthcare routines. The author does not accept responsibility for any liability, loss, or risk, personal or otherwise, incurred as a consequence of the use or application of any of the content in this book.

All healing practices, metaphysical perspectives, and energetic tools described are based on the author's professional experience, personal understanding, and spiritual philosophy. Results may vary. Readers are encouraged to use discernment and take full responsibility for their own wellbeing, choices, and experiences.

This book contains personal stories and client experiences. Where appropriate, identifying details have been changed to protect privacy and confidentiality.

The Time Paradox: Mastering Chronos and Kairos for a Life of Purpose

The goal of this book, The Time Paradox: Mastering Chronos and Kairos for a Life of Purpose, is to explore the profound influence of time, both measurable and experiential, on human potential, awareness, and alignment with purpose. In a culture driven by schedules and constant acceleration, this work offers a new lens through which to reclaim balance, clarity, and meaning.

We live between two dimensions of time: **Chronos**, the structured and mechanical measurement of moments, and **Kairos**, the intuitive rhythm of the soul where meaning arises beyond the clock. This book invites readers to master both, not by rejecting modern life, but by harmonizing its pace with the deeper intelligence of presence.

Through insights drawn from quantum biology, epigenetics, psychology, and the emerging science of consciousness, The Time Paradox examines how our perceptions of time shape the body, the mind, and the capacity to create. Each chapter explores a facet of this dynamic relationship, from the physiology of focus and the influence of emotion on energy, to the psychology of pace, the impact of technology, and the timeless potential within aging.

Across fourteen chapters, the book moves between scientific understanding and spiritual reflection, blending research with practice to help readers find equilibrium between performance and peace. It offers tools for cultivating flow, resilience, and awareness, while redefining what it means to live with purpose in an age that measures everything but presence.

Whether you are a thinker, creator, or seeker, The Time Paradox offers a new approach to living with intention:

- A focus that deepens rather than narrows.
- A pace that sustains rather than depletes.
- A presence that turns every moment into possibility.

Through the integration of science, philosophy, and the art of awareness, this book invites you to stop racing against time and begin to live within it. For when you align Chronos with Kairos, everything changes, your health, your focus, your purpose, and the way you experience life itself.

Susan L Williams

Table of Contents

Chapter 1: Introduction 1
Chapter 2: Chronos and Its Role in Modern Life 3
Chapter 3: Kairos: The Power of Opportunistic Time 9
Chapter 4: The Philosophical Foundations of Time 15
Chapter 5: Time Perception and Human Cognition 21
Chapter 6: Chronos in Professional Environments 27
Chapter 7: Using Kairos for Creative Breakthroughs 34
Chapter 8: Balancing Chronos & Kairos in Decisions 40
Chapter 9: Mastering Chronos to Build Focus 47
Chapter 10: Cultivating Kairos for Personal Growth & Fulfillment 54
Chapter 11: The Dynamics of Time in Relationships 60
Chapter 12: Technology, Time, & the Modern Dilemma 68
Chapter 13: Integrating Chronos & Kairos 75
Chapter 14: Timelessness and the Illusion of Age 81
Conclusion: Embracing the Paradox of Time 87
Appendix: Practical Exercises & Reflection Prompts 90

Chapter 1: Introduction

Time. We all know it, live by it, chase it, and sometimes feel chased by it. It marks our calendars, nudges our decisions, and wraps itself around every part of our lives. But for something so present, so constant, time is still one of those curious things that we don't really stop to question. Most of us think of time as minutes slipping by, deadlines approaching, or simply something we never have enough of.

But what if that's only one piece of the puzzle? What if time isn't just ticking clocks and rigid schedules? What if, by understanding it differently, we could begin to live not just more efficiently, but more fully?

That's the invitation this book extends. It's not your standard guide to cramming more into your day or finding clever hacks to juggle everything at once. Instead, it's a journey into the deeper qualities of time, the ones that don't always show up on a clock but are felt in quiet moments, in gut instincts, in those little nudges from life that seem to appear just when we need them.

Time, it turns out, has layers. Some push us to act, plan, and get things done. Others ask us to slow down, to listen, to notice. And when we ignore one side of that equation, life tends to feel off-kilter, rushed, drained, or just out of sync. But when we start to tune in, when we begin to recognize the richer dimensions of time, something shifts. Life starts to breathe differently.

Imagine being handed not just a planner or a to-do list, but a kind of inner compass, one that points to those moments when something more is possible. When the timing is right, not just in a practical sense, but in a soul-deep, "this is the moment" kind of way.

Why does any of this matter? Because for so many of us, life has become a blur of obligations, constant motion, and the nagging feeling that we're always behind. We've become experts at being busy, but not necessarily at being present, or fulfilled.

This book offers a new way to see and relate to time, not as something to battle against, but as something to align with. You'll meet ancient concepts, supported by modern insights, that challenge the idea that time is only ever linear or limited. And through them, you'll be invited to look at your own relationship with time, where it flows, where it sticks, and where it's asking you to pay attention.

These ideas aren't abstract; they're meant to be lived. When we begin to honour both the structured and the spontaneous aspects of time, we find a rhythm that makes sense for us. Sometimes that means acting fast, guided by a spark of intuition. Other times, it means taking things slow, building with intention and care.

This book follows that rhythm, starting with the time we all know - Chronos, the linear kind - before guiding you into the world of Kairos, the kind of time that holds magic, insight, and transformation.

It's not about rules or rigid systems. It's about learning to speak time's many languages, so you can dance with it instead of wrestle it.

Because in the end, time isn't the enemy. It's a companion, a mirror, a teacher, a space where your life unfolds. And when you learn to walk with it instead of run against it, everything changes.

Chapter 2: Chronos and Its Role in Modern Life

Chronos, that steady tick of the clock, quietly governs much of our everyday lives. It gives shape to our workdays, our routines, our deadlines. There's something powerful about its precision, something that can feel both supportive and, at times, a little suffocating. We're often taught to see time as a force to race against or something we need to outsmart, but Chronos isn't the enemy. In fact, it offers us a rhythm we can lean into. A rhythm that can help us build momentum and develop discipline in ways that truly serve us.

In a world where efficiency is worn like a badge of honor, understanding Chronos allows us to ride the current rather than be dragged by it. Whether you're a creative, a professional, or someone simply trying to navigate the demands of modern life, this linear flow of time can become a trusted guide. When we work with it, instead of against it, minutes and hours begin to carry more meaning. They become bricks in the foundation of something greater.

Used consciously, Chronos isn't just about measuring time. It becomes a tool for shaping life with more intention. It helps us focus. It clears space for steady progress. It reminds us that consistency matters. But here's the key: mastering Chronos isn't about becoming rigid. It's about learning its rhythm well enough that you can create room for the unexpected. That's where the magic often lives, just beyond the structure, in the moments we didn't plan for but are ready to receive.

Measuring Time: The Nature of Chronos

Time often feels like something we're trying to catch. No matter how tightly we hold on, it slips between our fingers, carrying the moments with it. The kind of time we usually think of - measured time - is what we've come to know as Chronos. This structured form gives our days a framework, a dependable outline that keeps the world in motion. It breaks life into clear pieces: seconds, minutes, hours. It's how we set appointments, meet deadlines, and organize just about every part of our modern lives.

From ancient sundials to the most advanced atomic clocks, we've always searched for ways to capture time with increasing accuracy. It speaks to our need for order and our belief that, by tracking time more precisely, we might somehow master it. And while this exactness has its benefits, there's more to Chronos than numbers. It quietly reminds us that time is not only a concept but a resource, limited, always moving, and shaped by the way we use it.

Chronos helps us move through our days with rhythm and structure. It influences how we set goals, how we build routines, and even how we understand our own progress. But it also carries a certain weight. Its movement is one-directional. Once a moment is gone, it cannot be reclaimed. This creates an ongoing pressure to perform, to stay ahead, to do more with less. In that push for efficiency, time can begin to feel like a force we're always chasing. It is in this quiet tension, the support of structure balanced against the pressure to keep up, that many of us begin to feel the strain.

Still, learning to understand Chronos is essential. It gives us the shared rhythm that keeps things flowing. Without it, nothing would connect. Flights wouldn't take off on time. Conversations across time zones would fall apart. Even something as simple as meeting a friend would feel uncertain. Chronos helps align our actions with others. It's the language of coordination, of planning, of commitment.

Now imagine a single day with no clocks, no schedules. It might sound freeing at first, but very quickly, it becomes hard to navigate.

There's no anchor. No common ground. We rely on Chronos to slice the passing of life into pieces we can actually use. It allows us to think in terms of beginnings and endings, of preparation and completion. In this way, Chronos gives our experiences a kind of storyline, even if it can't tell us what the story means.

That meaning is ours to bring. The clock might count each hour the same, but we know that not all hours feel equal. A quiet moment at sunrise is not the same as a tense meeting in a boardroom, even if both take sixty minutes. This is where understanding Chronos becomes more than just practical. It becomes personal. We start to notice how time feels, not just how it ticks.

Much of modern progress has been built around Chronos. During industrial times, workers showed up by the hour and machines ran on strict schedules. Today, our digital tools carry the same pattern forward. Software calendars, time trackers, alerts, reminders, they all help us manage our hours, but they also echo that old rhythm of keeping pace. For those building businesses or creative projects, this structure can be a gift. It offers guardrails for focus. It marks clear boundaries that keep ideas moving forward.

But structure isn't everything. The very tools that help us plan can also limit how we experience our time. When every moment is boxed in, we risk missing the ones that feel most alive. A calendar doesn't always know the value of stillness, or the sudden spark of inspiration. Chronos treats every minute the same, but life doesn't.

Even so, we can't dismiss the power of measured time. Its universal quality means we can collaborate across continents. It brings clarity. It reduces confusion. The shared system of hours and days lets us coordinate our lives with others in ways that would otherwise be impossible. And yet, within that same hour, two people might live completely different stories. One racing against a deadline, another lost in reflection. The structure stays the same, but the experience does not.

Chronos also brings with it a set of tools that shape both how we act and how we think. From clocks to calendars, from daily schedules to long-term plans, we've learned to map time in a way that lets us move confidently through the unknown. These tools are not just about marking events; they also help us imagine what could be. They turn vague ideas into clear intentions.

In work environments, this becomes especially clear. Deadlines, meetings, launch dates, all depend on Chronos. When used well, this structure keeps teams aligned and projects on track. But in more fluid parts of life - creative work, healing, personal growth - rigidity of measured time can feel like a poor fit. That doesn't make Chronos wrong. It just means that not all growth follows a timetable. True skill lies in knowing when to rely on structure and when to step back and allow space.

Chronos gives us a way to hold time in our hands, even if only briefly. It draws clear lines around beginnings and endings. It makes the invisible feel tangible. It offers us the gift of order. But it cannot tell us what matters most. That part is up to us.

When we truly understand Chronos, we stop trying to fight it. Instead, we learn to use it as a foundation. A base from which we can stretch, explore, and grow. Because the measured moments are not the whole story, but they are the canvas on which we paint our lives.

As we continue, we'll begin to explore how this structured sense of time interacts with something far more fluid. Those moments that don't fit neatly into boxes but arrive with unexpected significance. For now, let Chronos remind you that structure is not the enemy. It is the ground beneath your feet, the steady beat beneath the music of your life.

The Impact of Chronos on Productivity and Routine

In the fast-moving pace of daily life, Chronos quietly defines what we often call productivity. It shapes how we design our days, guiding the flow of meetings, deadlines, and the long lists of tasks that fill our calendars. This form of time, linear and measurable, marks progress with each tick forward. It is often seen as the ultimate measure of output and efficiency. But there is more to notice when we take a closer look at how this structure influences not just our actions but the texture of our routines.

For professionals, creatives, and lifelong learners who care about meaningful progress, understanding Chronos is not only about tracking hours. It is about recognizing the quiet pressures that come with this kind of measurement. Many of us have inherited a view of productivity that values speed and volume over depth and connection. While this mindset can certainly fuel results, it also risks creating a narrow path where schedules dominate and opportunities for richer engagement are overlooked.

One of the most noticeable effects of Chronos is how it splits our days into separate parts. Hours are assigned to specific activities - emails, focused work, exercise - and the result is often a string of disconnected segments. This compartmentalization can encourage a sense of urgency, which has the power to drive action but may also make it harder to feel present in any one task. The constant shifting of attention can blur the boundaries between meaningful effort and mechanical movement. Still, that same urgency can help us set goals and get things done, offering a structure that supports clarity and intention.

In the professional world, deadlines show how Chronos creates momentum. They provide focus, spark motivation, and draw clear lines around what needs to be completed. But they can also introduce stress, especially when the focus turns solely to finishing on time instead of caring about the quality or creative spark behind the work. Over time, this can chip away at motivation, replacing inspiration with a kind of transactional routine where time and output are constantly exchanged.

Routines, too, are built within the patterns of Chronos. Our bodies and minds often benefit from predictability, and structured habits can create a strong foundation. Whether that means waking at the same hour, setting aside time to move or meditate, or creating rituals for focused work, these rhythms help us stay anchored. But when routines become too rigid, they risk becoming cages. Energy, creativity, and curiosity do not always arrive on a schedule, and if every moment is pinned to the clock, burnout is never far behind.

Chronos brings order and reliability, but it does not define the quality of the time it structures. When used with care, it becomes a tool that serves our deeper intentions rather than a system that overrides them. The goal is not to escape structure but to use it as a container; one that holds our days in place while still allowing space to breathe.

Many creatives use strategies like time blocking to carve out protected time for deep work. These practices respect the rhythm of Chronos while also giving it direction and purpose. In this way, the clock becomes less of a burden and more of an ally. It signals focus, but it also sets boundaries that keep distractions at bay and preserve the energy needed for thoughtful creation.

That said, living too closely tied to the clock can lead to scattered focus. The digital world is full of alerts, messages, and requests that interrupt our attention. Time moves forward, but we often find ourselves jumping between tasks without finishing any one of them fully. Here, the influence of Chronos can backfire. What is meant to bring structure ends up fragmenting our experience, leaving us more tired and less productive.

This is why many productivity thinkers speak to the difference between being busy and being purposeful. Filling every hour does not mean we are making progress. What matters more is how aligned those actions are with what we value. Chronos can support this alignment when we use it to guide intentional choices rather than to simply react to what is urgent.

Much of modern life reflects an unconscious trust in Chronos. Alarm clocks wake us, meetings are set to the hour, and breaks are often timed rather than felt. These external cues are helpful, but if we rely on them too heavily without checking in with our inner rhythms, we risk becoming disconnected from ourselves. The result is often a cycle of overwork followed by exhaustion. Our energy may rise and fall, but the clock keeps ticking, indifferent to our internal state.

Even rest becomes something to schedule. In fast-paced cultures, downtime often turns into a block on a calendar rather than a space to truly let go. Without intentional space for recovery, rest can lose its power. It becomes a task instead of a source of renewal. Over time, this erodes our capacity to sustain effort, even if our calendar looks full of well-ordered days.

Chronos also operates at a collective level. Organizations, institutions, and communities depend on shared schedules to coordinate work and measure results. Weekly targets, quarterly goals, and annual reviews are all rooted in the framework of measured time. This creates stability and fairness in many ways, but it can also limit creative exploration. When everything must fit a timeline, the unexpected often gets lost.

Becoming more aware of Chronos allows us to design better routines. Ones that listen to both structure and flow. We might notice that our energy peaks in the morning or that creative insights come more easily after a break. Aligning tasks with these patterns helps reduce friction and increase fulfillment. This way, Chronos supports not only productivity but also well-being.

A mindful relationship with Chronos invites us to shape our experience of time from the inside out. Rather than being pushed forward by endless deadlines, we begin to choose how we meet the day. Structure becomes a frame, not a cage. Routine becomes a rhythm, not a rule.

Chronos offers clarity. It helps us mark progress, meet goals, and stay organized. But it does not have to run the whole show. It is possible to live with structure while also staying open to those moments that do not fit the clock but still matter deeply.

When we approach time this way, it no longer feels like something to outrun. It becomes something we can work with. Not to control every second, but to move through our days with presence and care. Chronos becomes a scaffold for creativity, growth, and meaning. Not because it measures everything, but because it gives us the space to decide what matters most.

Chapter 3: Kairos: The Power of Opportunistic Time

Where Chronos offers a steady, measurable beat, Kairos introduces something else entirely. It is a rhythm we feel rather than count - a sense that the moment is ripe, that something important is ready to unfold. This kind of time cannot be planned for in the traditional sense. It arrives quietly, often without warning, and calls for our full attention.

Kairos is that opening when readiness meets opportunity. It might last a second or stretch into something longer, but its essence is the same - a chance to act, create, or shift something in a meaningful way. These moments carry a kind of weight that clocks and calendars can't account for. They ask us to listen more closely, not to schedules, but to what life is offering right now.

To live with an awareness of Kairos is to step beyond deadlines and routine. It means becoming more attuned to timing that doesn't come from a clock, but from within. This kind of awareness can't be forced. It's cultivated slowly, through presence, reflection, and a willingness to pause long enough to recognize when the conditions are right.

For professionals, creatives, and anyone seeking meaningful progress, Kairos is not about luck. It's about developing a kind of sensitivity - a readiness to respond when the moment calls. These moments often appear quietly, between the lines of a structured day - in a passing thought, a conversation that lingers, or an idea that arrives uninvited but refuses to leave.

Kairos invites us to move with life, not just through it. It reminds us that some of our most important steps forward do not come from following a plan, but from recognizing the moment when something deeper is possible. In this way, Kairos reshapes how we think about growth, productivity, and the pace of our lives. It encourages a kind of flow that honors both preparation and spontaneity, helping us meet life not with control, but with presence.

Defining Kairos in Modern Life and Practice

When most people think of time, they imagine the measurable kind - clocks, calendars, and schedules that structure our days. This is **Chronos**, the time of progress charts, to-do lists, and deadlines. Yet beyond this structured flow lies another dimension of time that can't be captured by numbers alone. This is **Kairos**: the felt sense of the right moment, when action aligns naturally with purpose and energy.

In essence, Kairos is about timing that resonates. It's the experience of *knowing* when the conditions are right - when insight lands, a conversation opens, or a decision feels undeniably ready. Unlike Chronos, which is quantitative, Kairos is qualitative. Its value isn't in how much time passes, but in how fully present and attuned we are when it does.

Modern thinkers often describe Kairos as a state of alignment rather than a specific instant. In creative work, it's the flow moment when ideas connect effortlessly. In relationships, it's the pause that allows empathy to surface before responding. In leadership, it's the ability to sense readiness - when a team, market, or idea finally clicks into coherence.

Psychology and neuroscience now echo what ancient intuition already knew: the brain and body register timing cues long before conscious thought. Subtle signals - body tension, tone of voice, shifts in attention - inform whether we're in sync with the moment or pushing against it. Kairos, then, isn't mystical; it's an attunement we can strengthen. Training presence, deep listening, and emotional regulation increases our ability to recognize and act on these windows of opportunity.

In modern mindfulness, Kairos appears as the practice of pausing. Not idle waiting, but a deliberate slowing down to sense what's unfolding. When you stop rushing to fill every gap, you begin to notice timing that's already speaking. The right insight, phrase, or step forward often arises in that space - not forced but allowed.

This perspective changes how we define success with time. Chronos rewards consistency and order; Kairos rewards awareness and trust. Together, they create a balanced rhythm - one that allows disciplined effort to coexist with intuition and flow. The art lies in knowing when to shift gears: when to stay steady in structure, and when to release control so new possibilities can emerge.

Consider how this plays out in daily life. A manager senses the perfect moment to share an idea that had stalled before. A teacher pauses mid-lesson and shifts direction because the room's energy has changed. A runner feels the instant when their stride becomes effortless. These aren't accidents; they're examples of Kairos - moments when awareness meets readiness.

Across cultures, this sense of right timing shows up under many names: in Japanese philosophy as *ma* (the space between things), in African wisdom traditions as the "now that carries power," and in Indigenous teachings as moving with the cycles of nature rather than forcing them. These traditions all point to the same truth - that timing has depth, not just duration.

In today's over-scheduled world, Kairos becomes an act of resistance against constant acceleration. It reminds us that productivity without presence leads to burnout, while presence without direction can lose focus. When we learn to balance both, time becomes not something we chase but something we participate in.

Ultimately, Kairos calls us to live with discernment. It invites us to listen for when effort should give way to ease, when planning should pause for insight, and when a fleeting opportunity deserves our full attention. It's a skill, not a mystery - one that grows through practice, reflection, and a willingness to trust the natural rhythm of time itself.

Recognizing Kairos Moments in Daily Life

In the steady rhythm of clocks and the ongoing structure of daily routines, it is easy to miss the subtle moments that carry deeper meaning. These are not simply points on a timeline. They are Kairos moments - instances where time feels different, where something shifts and possibility opens. Unlike the measured steps of Chronos, Kairos reveals itself when the conditions are just right and calls us to act with presence and intention. These moments are not about duration. They are about depth.

Kairos does not arrive with noise or urgency. It often hides in the quiet spaces - a conversation that suddenly turns, an insight that surfaces while doing something ordinary, a moment of clarity that breaks through distraction. These openings ask us to respond before they pass. And they will pass. To recognize them, we need more than awareness. We need attunement. We need to become sensitive to the rhythms of life that live beyond the clock.

Each day holds these possibilities. They may appear during a routine meeting or while walking through a familiar space. What matters is not the setting, but your readiness to notice. Perhaps it's a fleeting thought worth exploring, or a shared silence that holds more truth than words. Kairos moments often feel like pauses - charged with potential, asking for your attention. When you begin to recognize them, your relationship with time changes. You start to feel more connected, more in sync with the present moment.

This kind of awareness does not come from tracking the time. It comes from listening. It means tuning in to your surroundings, your relationships, and your own internal signals. A sudden shift in emotion, a moment of focus, or even a physical sensation can signal that something important is forming. For professionals and creatives, these Kairos moments might appear as flashes of clarity or instinctive leaps - the right idea at the right time, or a conversation that moves something forward unexpectedly.

Mindfulness is a key to developing this sensitivity. You do not need to abandon structure, but rather learn to inhabit it more fully. Being present in your daily routines allows you to notice when something shifts beneath the surface. You might be in motion - answering emails, attending meetings, crossing off tasks - and still sense when a moment opens into something more. That opening, however small, may offer a new way forward.

Kairos also speaks through the body. A quickened heartbeat, a surge of energy, or a calm that arrives suddenly can signal alignment. These responses do not always make logical sense at first, but they matter. They often arise just before insight, just before a decision, just before an action that changes everything. Learning to trust these cues is part of learning to live with Kairos.

Across work and creativity, these moments have the power to spark breakthroughs. They help shift perspective, solve challenges, or breathe life into an idea that felt stuck. But they often require space. If your schedule is too tight or your attention too divided, they may pass unnoticed. Pausing, even briefly, can make space for Kairos to land.

Reflection is a valuable tool here. Journaling small moments, surprising thoughts, or meaningful encounters helps bring patterns into focus. You begin to notice what leads up to a Kairos experience and how it tends to arrive. With time, you become more familiar with the conditions that support it - quiet, curiosity, trust. It stops being rare and starts becoming part of how you live.

Kairos also plays a powerful role in relationships. A conversation held at the right moment can build trust or open new connection. A kind gesture offered without delay can shift the tone of an entire exchange. These moments require discernment. They ask us to read both the situation and ourselves clearly. Emotional intelligence deepens with

Kairos awareness. It brings warmth and precision to how we relate to others.

Not every opening is a true Kairos moment. Some opportunities are distractions in disguise. The difference lies in how it feels. A Kairos moment carries a sense of alignment - a quiet rightness, not a rush of urgency. The action it calls for may still be bold, but it does not come from pressure. It comes from presence. Learning to distinguish these moments takes practice, and part of that practice involves knowing when to wait.

Life does not follow a fixed script. Its timing often surprises us. That is why flexibility is so important. Structure gives us a foundation, but too much rigidity can shut the door on something unexpected. When we remain open to shifting course or pausing briefly, we create space for Kairos to arrive. This is where the richness often lives - just outside what we had planned.

Living with Kairos means no longer seeing time as something to endure or control. Instead, time becomes a space where meaningful choices can unfold. The sense of agency grows. You begin to see each day not just as a list of tasks, but as a series of openings. Each Kairos moment becomes a pivot - not just for progress, but for deeper connection, greater clarity, or personal renewal.

In the end, learning to recognize Kairos changes your relationship with yourself. It invites you to live with attention and intention. It asks you to stay present to the rhythms that don't always follow logic but still lead somewhere important. This way of being does not require perfection. It simply asks that you notice. That you respond when something within you says, "this matters now."

Kairos is not a rare visitor. It is always moving through our lives. The more we pay attention, the more we begin to meet it. Not with force, but with readiness. Not with control, but with care. And in doing so, we come into closer relationship with time itself - not just as a system to manage, but as a living context for growth, connection, and change.

Chapter 4: The Philosophical Foundations of Time

As we continue exploring Chronos and Kairos, it becomes important to look at the deeper roots that shape how we understand time itself. Time is not just a series of scheduled hours or brief moments that pass us by. It is a concept that has stirred thought across cultures and generations. Philosophers, spiritual teachers, and scientists alike have asked not only what time is, but how we experience it.

In many Western traditions, time is often seen as linear. It moves from past to present to future - a sequence of events connected by cause and effect. This perspective supports planning, order, and a clear sense of direction. It helps build systems and structures that rely on predictable progress.

In contrast, many Eastern philosophies offer a more cyclical view. Time is seen as flowing in patterns, connected through repetition and return. Seasons, life cycles, and natural rhythms are central to this understanding. Instead of focusing solely on forward motion, these traditions emphasize harmony between inner awareness and the movement of life around us.

Both of these perspectives offer something valuable. The linear view helps us build and organize. The cyclical view reminds us to reflect, reset, and stay grounded in the present. Together, they offer a fuller picture - one that acknowledges both movement and rhythm, progress and pause.

To work well with time, we need both. Chronos provides the structure that helps us act. Kairos adds depth and meaning to those actions. One gives form, the other gives texture. When we begin to see time in this layered way, we shift from simply managing our days to engaging with them more consciously.

This philosophical foundation is not just an intellectual exercise. It invites a different way of living. It helps us move from reaction to reflection, from doing to being aware of why we do. It is the difference between filling a schedule and choosing how we want to experience the time we have.

Understanding time in this deeper way does more than support productivity. It encourages intentionality. It helps us shape our lives with care, weaving together discipline and presence. This is how time becomes more than something we track. It becomes something we live with awareness.

Historical Perspectives on Chronos and Kairos

To truly understand our relationship with time, it helps to look back at how early cultures made sense of it. The Greeks gave us two distinct concepts that still carry weight today: Chronos and Kairos. These weren't abstract theories for them. They shaped how people made decisions, approached meaning, and responded to the unfolding of life. Chronos represented the structured, sequential nature of time - the version we track with clocks and calendars. Kairos, by contrast, spoke to the quality of time - the moment when something feels ready, significant, or ripe for action.

Chronos is often seen as the more familiar of the two. It moves in a straight line, carving time into past, present, and future. For the Greeks, this was the dimension that made it possible to organize society - to schedule rituals, guide farming cycles, and coordinate shared life.

Chronos gave rise to the systems we still rely on today, from the calendar to the atomic clock. It offered predictability, and in many ways, it became the skeleton around which the rest of life was structured.

But even then, Chronos was never seen as the full story. Alongside this steady, measurable time was something more fleeting - Kairos. It described the moment when everything lines up, when action taken has power beyond its timing on a clock. In speech, it was the perfect pause before the right word. In decision-making, it was the sense that now is the time. Kairos asked not how long something took, but whether the moment had arrived.

These concepts show up in early Greek literature and philosophy. Chronos appears in depictions of the cosmos, often associated with vast, unstoppable flow. Kairos, though less visible, had an equally powerful presence. He was imagined as a figure with wings on his feet, a lock of hair on his forehead, and a bald head in back - a vivid image that symbolized how you had to catch opportunity while it was in front of you, before it moved on. The message was simple and enduring: some moments matter more than others, and you need to be present enough to see them.

This duality between Chronos and Kairos reflected not just two kinds of time, but two different ways of living. Chronos belonged to the outer world - schedules, routines, and linear progression. Kairos belonged to the inner world - intuition, readiness, and sensing the right moment to engage. The Greeks understood that fulfillment came not from structure alone, but from the ability to navigate between these dimensions.

Philosophers carried this awareness forward. Aristotle spoke of Kairos in his reflections on rhetoric. He pointed out that even the best idea, if shared at the wrong time, would fall flat. He emphasized timing as a form of wisdom - knowing when to speak, when to act, and how to match your message to the moment. His insight continues to resonate, especially in a world where good ideas are not enough unless they land when people are ready to hear them.

Chronos, with its precision, appeals to reason. Kairos appeals to something less easily defined. In ancient Greece, awareness of Kairos was often considered a spiritual discipline - a way of aligning with nature, with self, and with something larger than either. Kairos asked for presence. It required listening, sensing, and responding in a way that felt deeply human.

As Western culture evolved, so did its relationship to time. With the rise of science and industry, Chronos became dominant. Time was measured in tighter and tighter increments. Schedules became central. Productivity was defined by how much could be achieved in how little time. And while this brought remarkable advances, it also narrowed the way many people related to time - reducing it to a resource to manage or a pressure to endure.

Still, Kairos never disappeared. It remained alive in creativity, in leadership, in spiritual life. Great leaders, artists, and innovators often speak of sensing when the time is right - not based on analysis alone, but on a deeper kind of attunement. This ability to recognize Kairos shows up in moments of insight, in acts of courage, in decisions that shape lives and history.

Other cultures have held onto similar concepts. In Chinese philosophy, the idea of "shiji" describes the decisive moment when timing becomes everything. Many Indigenous traditions speak of living in rhythm with natural cycles, waiting for signs that the time is right to move or act. These ways of knowing reflect a shared understanding: that time is not only something to count, but something to feel.

In today's world, many people live caught in the structure of Chronos - managing deadlines, filling schedules, and racing the clock. But the breakthroughs often happen elsewhere. Insight, creativity, and growth arise in Kairos moments. They come not from following the script, but from stepping into something that cannot be planned. When we begin to notice these moments, we expand our capacity to live more fully.

Importantly, Chronos and Kairos are not enemies. They are partners. Chronos provides the structure that holds our days. Kairos brings the energy that transforms them. The challenge is not choosing one over the other, but learning how to move between them. When you build structure without losing your sense of timing - when you hold space for both planning and intuition - your relationship with time begins to shift.

This deeper awareness helps us reframe time itself. Rather than seeing it as a container for tasks, we start to see it as a living experience - one shaped by rhythm, attention, and choice. Time becomes something we participate in, not just something we chase.

In the end, returning to these ancient ideas gives us more than historical insight. It offers tools for modern life. Chronos gives us order. Kairos gives us opportunity. Together, they invite us to approach time not just with discipline, but with presence. And in doing so, they help us shape lives that are not only efficient, but meaningful.

Time in Western and Eastern Philosophies

The idea of time has fascinated thinkers across cultures for thousands of years. But the way time is understood has not always followed the same path. Western and Eastern traditions have approached it through distinctly different perspectives. In the West, time is often seen as a straight line - a clear sequence from past to present to future. This view supports the way modern life is organized, with clocks, calendars, and schedules providing structure and predictability. But this linear approach can also create pressure. It reduces time to something we must use wisely or risk wasting, turning it into a resource that demands constant attention.

In many Eastern traditions, time is viewed differently. Instead of a strict line, it is often seen as fluid and cyclical. Rather than focusing on steady forward motion, these philosophies speak to patterns, rhythms, and a sense of return. Time is not something to conquer, but something to live with. This view encourages presence, patience, and alignment with natural flow, rather than urgency or control. When we place these two approaches side by side, the contrast becomes clear. Western thought emphasizes measurable progress. Eastern thought invites attunement. And within that contrast lies an opportunity to find a deeper, more balanced way to live with time.

In Western philosophy, thinkers like Aristotle and Augustine shaped our early understanding. Aristotle described time as a way of measuring change - something we track in order to understand what comes before and what follows. It was, in his view, tied to motion and sequence. Augustine, while more introspective, still imagined time as a kind of flow that the mind tries to grasp. He noticed that as soon as the present arrives, it begins to slip into the past, while the future remains just out of reach. Even with this reflective insight, time was still anchored in a forward-moving framework, deeply influenced by both religious and rational ideas of purpose.

Centuries later, with the rise of modern science, this approach grew even stronger. Thinkers like Newton defined time as absolute - a fixed backdrop against which all things unfold. This gave birth to the kind of precise timekeeping we now rely on in everything from global communication to industrial systems. It also shaped the way professional life operates today, especially in cultures that value efficiency and productivity. But in this model, the lived experience of time - how it feels, how it moves through us - is often left out.

Eastern traditions offer another path. In Hindu thought, time is seen as cyclical and infinite. Creation, destruction, and renewal are part of an ongoing rhythm. These cycles are vast, spanning cosmic eras, yet they also mirror everyday life. Time is not about strict progression, but about understanding the patterns in which life unfolds. There is wisdom in waiting, in returning, in seeing every ending as part of a larger beginning.

In Buddhism, time is closely tied to perception. It is not an objective force but something shaped by awareness. The present moment becomes the center of experience, fleeting yet full. Through practices like meditation, attention returns to the now - the only place where change can actually occur. This approach breaks down the urgency of past and future. It encourages presence, spaciousness, and the idea that transformation happens not by rushing forward, but by showing up fully in each moment.

Taoism adds another layer to this picture. Time is not something to push against, but something to flow with. The Tao describes a natural order that moves without effort. In this view, trying to control time leads to resistance. Moving with it leads to harmony. Just like a river, time flows whether we grasp at it or not. Learning to move with its current can bring ease, wisdom, and clarity. This perspective teaches that both stillness and action have their place. Each is part of the larger rhythm of life.

Taken together, these perspectives show us two different but complementary truths. Western traditions give us tools for structure, planning, and progress. Eastern traditions remind us to listen, to slow down, and to move with intention. Neither view is complete on its own. But together, they open space for a richer relationship with time - one that supports both doing and being.

For professionals, creatives, and anyone seeking meaningful growth, this balance is powerful. The ability to plan and execute with clarity, rooted in the structure of Chronos, helps move work forward. But without space for intuition and timing - the essence of Kairos - that same structure can become confining. Insight, creativity, and renewal often happen in the spaces where we let go of the clock and pay attention to what is actually unfolding.

This kind of integration reflects a growing shift in how we relate to time. More people are recognizing that time is not just something to manage. It is something to experience. When we see time as both measurable and meaningful, we give ourselves more ways to move through complexity. We become more adaptive, more resilient, and more open to what each moment offers.

This shift begins with awareness. It means noticing not only what we are doing, but how we are relating to time while doing it. Are we pushing forward without pause? Or are we allowing room for timing, flow, and presence? Expanding our view of time makes it possible to blend structure with softness - to meet deadlines while also protecting space for reflection and rest.

In practice, this could look like designing schedules that hold time for both focus and openness. It might involve planning ahead while also leaving space for spontaneity. It may mean trusting that rest is not wasted time, but necessary for creativity to emerge. These changes don't require abandoning structure. They ask only that we hold it more lightly and more consciously.

The wisdom of both East and West can serve as a guide. Chronos gives us a framework. Kairos invites us into possibility. One helps us move forward. The other helps us know when to act. Together, they offer a map for living with purpose and clarity - not just to keep up, but to move through time with presence and intention.

Chapter 5: Time Perception and Human Cognition

How we perceive time influences far more than just our ability to keep a schedule. It shapes how we think, how we remember, and how we make decisions. Time is not just something that happens outside of us. Our minds are constantly interpreting it - blending the steady rhythm of the clock with a more internal sense of when something feels right. In this way, Chronos and Kairos are not just external forces. They live in how we experience each day.

Sometimes a moment feels expansive, as if time has slowed down. Other times, hours pass unnoticed in the blur of distraction. These shifts point to a simple but powerful truth: our perception of time is deeply tied to attention, emotion, and mental engagement. When we are present, time stretches. When we are scattered, it slips away. This inner experience is not separate from how we live. It is part of the way time actually unfolds for us.

By paying attention to this psychological rhythm, we gain the ability to work with time more intentionally. Chronos offers structure, helping us stay on track and follow through. Kairos speaks through instinct and timing - moments when something just feels ready. Together, they form a complete picture. One helps us organize. The other helps us respond.

Learning how the mind interacts with time opens the door to greater clarity and insight. It invites us to design our days in a way that supports both focus and flow. We begin to notice when our energy peaks, when attention drifts, and when creativity sparks without warning. Instead of fighting these rhythms, we learn to follow them. We make space for moments that are not only efficient, but meaningful.

This shift does not require abandoning structure. It asks for more awareness within it. When we tune in to how time feels - not just how it moves on a clock - we start to act with more presence. We recognize that some of our most important breakthroughs do not arrive on schedule. They arrive when we are open, when we are aligned, when something within says now.

Understanding time through both Chronos and Kairos allows us to meet life more fully. It encourages a way of living where structure supports spontaneity, and routine makes room for insight. In this space, creativity deepens, focus becomes more natural, and growth feels more sustainable. We are not simply managing time. We are engaging with it as something alive - something that responds to how we show up.

How We Experience Chronos and Kairos Mentally

Time moves through our minds in more than one dimension. We experience both Chronos - the structured, clock-bound time - and Kairos - the opportune moment that feels charged with significance. Together, these dimensions shape how we think, decide, and engage with daily life. Chronos brings order and structure. Kairos brings timing and presence. Understanding this dual experience is essential, especially when we're looking to balance productivity with depth, planning with openness.

Chronos naturally draws the mind toward sequence and control. It speaks to the part of us that thrives on structure, clarity, and measurable progress. This makes sense. Human survival depended on tracking time for practical needs - anticipating weather, hunting, planting, and navigating seasonal patterns. Our brains adapted to this. They became finely attuned to rhythm, duration, and forward movement. Today, this shows up when we check the clock, plan our days in blocks, and create timelines to guide progress. The mind often finds comfort here. It builds systems. It anticipates what's ahead. It seeks mastery through predictability.

But this same mental orientation can tighten. Chronos can become a pressure. We begin to feel that time is always running out, that every minute must be accounted for. The ticking clock becomes a source of urgency. This view narrows our focus. It turns time into something to beat or manage rather than something to engage with meaningfully. The more we grip time this way, the more easily we slip into stress, routine, and a kind of mental constriction.

Kairos, by contrast, enters quietly. It is not driven by measurement but by sensing. It invites a different kind of attention - one that is tuned to the moment rather than the schedule. When Kairos arrives, it doesn't always make logical sense. It arrives as a shift in energy, a sense that now is the moment to speak, to act, to create. The mind here is not calculating. It is listening. It feels the opportunity before it can be explained. This kind of awareness is harder to train, but it brings depth and clarity that structure alone can't produce.

Mentally, Kairos feels spacious. It pulls us into the present without force. It does not require urgency, but it does require presence. The experience often feels like alignment - a quiet recognition that something is ready. There's often emotion tied to it - a sense of meaning, clarity, or connection. These moments stay with us. They linger in memory, not because they were long, but because they were full.

Kairos tends to show up when we are open. It often appears during moments of reflection, creativity, or connection. A flash of insight. A surprising solution. A conversation that deepens in an unexpected way. These are not accidents. They are the mind responding to subtle signals - both internal and external - that say something important is happening.

At times, Chronos and Kairos feel like they are pulling us in different directions. One pushes forward. The other invites us to pause. Chronos structures our work, our goals, our daily flow. Kairos adds texture, helping us know when to act and when to wait. Yet in modern culture, Chronos often takes the lead. We are trained to honor time that can be counted, not time that is felt. As a result, many of us lose contact with the subtler rhythm Kairos offers.

Interestingly, recent neuroscience helps shed light on this contrast. Chronos seems to involve brain regions linked to planning, sequencing, and executive function - areas that help us create order and stay on task. Kairos, on the other hand, is connected to emotional insight, holistic thinking, and intuitive awareness. These systems don't work against each other. They operate in parallel. But they speak different languages. One measures. The other senses.

You can think of them as two modes of consciousness. The Chronos mode organizes and builds. The Kairos mode listens and responds. Being able to move between these modes - or blend them - is a powerful skill. It gives us flexibility. It makes us more aware of timing, not just in terms of the clock, but in terms of what a situation truly needs.

Chronos also shapes memory. We often recall events based on their sequence - this happened, then that. Our minds build stories through timelines. This is grounding. It helps us make sense of what happened and how we got here. But Kairos memories feel different. They are anchored not in order, but in impact. A single moment might hold meaning far beyond its duration. These are the moments we describe as turning points. They live in us because of how they felt, not how long they lasted.

Accessing Kairos requires something that is increasingly rare in modern life - slowing down. Stillness. Reflection. These states allow the mind to soften its grip on control and open to what is actually happening. In that space, we start to sense timing differently. We become more attuned to subtle openings and more willing to follow where they lead.

Emotion also plays a role. Chronos can bring pressure, frustration, and even fear - especially when we feel there's never enough time. Kairos tends to bring connection, insight, and a sense of possibility. This contrast shapes not only how we use time, but how we feel about it. It affects creativity, decision-making, and overall well-being.

People who learn to work with both dimensions often describe moments of breakthrough - times when they were so immersed in the present that time seemed to disappear. Ironically, by letting go of the clock, they accessed something timeless. This is what Kairos offers - not the removal of time, but a richer, more vivid experience of it.

Still, this is not about choosing one over the other. Chronos helps us stay grounded. Kairos helps us stay open. Chronos provides structure. Kairos reveals meaning. We need both. Without Kairos, time becomes mechanical. Without Chronos, time becomes unanchored. The mental challenge is in learning to hold both - to use structure without being trapped by it, and to remain open without drifting.

Ultimately, how we experience time in the mind shapes how we live it. Building awareness of both Chronos and Kairos helps us notice when we are stuck in urgency and when an opportunity is quietly calling. It encourages a way of thinking that is both focused and flexible - one that supports growth, creativity, and connection.

When we learn to listen to how time moves within us, we stop treating it only as something to manage. We begin to treat it as something to live. This shift brings us closer to a life guided by both clarity and presence - a way of being where time becomes a tool, a teacher, and a companion in our unfolding path.

Psychological Effects of Time Awareness

Time awareness is more than simply knowing the hour or marking days on a calendar. It reaches deeper, shaping how we think, how we feel, and how we move through the world. When we become consciously aware of time - whether it's the steady rhythm of the clock or the arrival of a meaningful moment - we start to see how time not only structures our external lives but also influences our internal landscape. It becomes a lens through which we filter perception, emotion, and decision. In this way, time awareness is not passive. It plays an active role in shaping our mental and emotional experience.

Think about how it feels to work under the weight of a deadline. The sensation can be sharp and focused - a combination of urgency and alertness. This state tightens our focus, narrows attention, and fuels action. The brain responds quickly, often with a surge of adrenaline, preparing us to meet the task. This kind of pressure can be useful in small doses, but when it becomes constant, it begins to drain rather than energize. Time, when framed only as something we must beat or control, begins to wear down rather than lift up. What this reveals is how closely time awareness is tied to stress, motivation, and cognitive performance.

But when we shift from measuring time to sensing it - when we move from Chronos to Kairos - our awareness begins to soften. The internal experience expands. The mind becomes more open. In these moments, time often feels elastic. Seconds seem to stretch. Distractions fade. Presence deepens. This is the state many describe as "flow" or "being in the zone" - when the mind fully meets the moment, and creativity, insight, or ease naturally follow. These states are not just pleasant. They are often transformative. And they show us that time is not just about quantity. It also carries quality.

Time awareness also influences how we remember and how we imagine. Our sense of self is woven through time - through memory, reflection, and anticipation. We revisit the past to understand who we are. We project forward to shape what comes next. This ability to mentally move through time helps us learn, grow, and plan. But it can also trap us. When we dwell too long on regret or fixate on an uncertain future, time becomes heavy. The challenge is in staying connected to the present while still honoring the stories that shape us. A balanced awareness helps keep this process constructive. It allows us to carry the past with insight, and face the future with steadiness.

There is also a powerful connection between time awareness and our sense of control. When we feel in charge of our time, we often feel grounded. Autonomy grows. Clarity returns. But when time feels scarce or shaped entirely by external demands, it can leave us feeling helpless or scattered. This tension - between control and surrender - runs through much of modern life. Learning to move between these two states with some flexibility is essential for mental well-being and for sustaining purposeful action.

Time awareness also shapes what we pay attention to. The mind is always filtering - deciding what's urgent, what's important, and what can wait. When time feels abundant, space opens up. Curiosity returns. Longer-term thinking becomes possible. But when time feels tight, that space narrows. Attention shifts toward immediate concerns, often at the cost of depth or creativity. This is not just about efficiency. It's about how time perception quietly governs the quality of focus and emotional tone that we bring into our days.

On a social level, time awareness influences how we interact with others. Every culture holds shared ideas about time - ideas that affect how we communicate, collaborate, and connect. Punctuality, pacing, deadlines, and the tempo of conversation all reflect cultural values around time. When our personal rhythms align with these expectations, things often flow more easily. But when they diverge, tension can build. Misalignment may lead to misunderstanding or disconnection. This shared aspect of time reminds us that time is not only individual. It's relational. It's something we co-create through interaction and mutual expectation.

The more we explore this dynamic, the clearer it becomes that time awareness is both powerful and delicate. It offers the chance to plan, to prepare, and to reflect - but it also requires care. When taken to an extreme, time consciousness can foster anxiety, comparison, and a sense of never being "caught up." The antidote lies not in ignoring time, but in approaching it more mindfully. When we learn to see time as both structured and spacious - both measurable and meaningful - we begin to access a deeper kind of balance.

This mindset is not about favoring Chronos or Kairos. It's about understanding how they work together. Chronos helps us organize and commit. Kairos helps us notice and respond. When we become aware of how time shapes our thoughts and emotions, we begin to respond with more intention. We move from reacting to choosing. This ability to shift perspective and find rhythm is part of what builds resilience and creativity.

Developing this kind of awareness doesn't happen automatically. It takes practice. Small habits can help - pausing to reflect on how time is being felt in a moment, noticing emotional responses to deadlines or delays, or simply taking time to acknowledge the passing of a meaningful moment. Journaling, silence, and mindful breathing can all create space where awareness begins to grow. Over time, this attention forms a more intuitive relationship with time - one that is grounded, reflective, and alive.

In the end, time awareness is less about managing the clock and more about listening to how time moves through you. It's about noticing the emotional weight time carries, the stories we build from it, and the energy it brings to our choices. When we engage with time this way, it becomes something more than a schedule. It becomes a partner in presence. It becomes a way of living with clarity, attention, and care.

Chapter 6: Chronos in Professional Environments

In professional settings, Chronos often sets the pace. Deadlines mark key targets. Schedules give shape to the day. Meetings, timelines, and project milestones unfold in a clear, linear rhythm. This structured time helps coordinate work, track progress, and ensure accountability. It offers a shared framework that allows teams to function with consistency and focus. In this way, Chronos plays a necessary role in the flow of modern work.

But when Chronos is overemphasized, the structure it provides can begin to feel rigid. The very systems meant to support productivity may start to limit it. A constant focus on efficiency and output can crowd out creativity and depth. The pressure to keep up can lead to stress, fatigue, and a narrow view of success based solely on speed or volume. Over time, this mindset can disconnect people from the purpose and energy that first inspired their work.

Respecting Chronos as a tool - rather than submitting to it as a rule - becomes essential. Time structures are helpful when they serve clarity and alignment. But they are most effective when paired with space for reflection, adaptation, and presence. Professionals who learn to navigate both structure and flexibility often discover more sustainable rhythms. They stay accountable without becoming mechanical. They plan carefully but remain open to insight and change.

This balance invites a different relationship with time - one where discipline supports freedom, and where progress includes not only movement but meaning. When people feel empowered to engage time with intention, it stops being just a boundary. It becomes a framework that holds space for both productivity and presence. And in that space, work becomes not only more effective, but more fulfilling.

Scheduling, Deadlines, and Linear Time Management

In professional life, time is often treated as a linear resource - segmented into hours, minutes, and seconds, each designated for a specific task or outcome. This mindset is grounded in Chronos, the steady unfolding of clock time that supports scheduling, coordination, and predictability. Within organizations, deadlines and calendars act as scaffolding, holding together the flow of work and guiding teams through shared timelines. This structure provides clarity in environments that might otherwise feel chaotic. It allows projects to move forward, keeps responsibilities aligned, and offers a clear view of progress.

But structure alone is not without its limitations. While the framework of Chronos helps organize complex efforts, overreliance on it can narrow our engagement with time. Scheduling, for instance, serves as a tool for converting intention into action. It turns abstract goals into time-bound commitments. Yet, the act of breaking the day into blocks can also fragment experience, reducing time to a series of tasks rather than a lived process. This fragmentation can lead to disconnection - not only from our work, but from the deeper purpose that motivates it.

Linear time management does offer important benefits. It encourages focus. It supports accountability. Deadlines create direction and momentum. But when they become too rigid, they can foster stress and resistance. When deadlines feel imposed rather than aligned, they risk pulling us away from creative flow. The pressure to meet external benchmarks may crowd out internal signals that guide quality, insight, or timing. Chronos helps keep the wheels turning, but people are not machines. We need room for responsiveness and reflection.

Professional culture often reinforces this focus on output and adherence. Time becomes something to manage, to track, or to race against. Productivity is measured in units - hours logged, tasks completed, milestones hit. This measurement helps evaluate progress, but it can also create a narrow sense of success. In the push for completion, we may overlook the moments where deeper value resides - moments of pause, insight, or redirection. Time begins to feel transactional, rather than transformational.

Still, the benefits of scheduling are real. In any shared endeavor, timelines help align efforts and build trust. Deadlines support coordination. Time frames allow for resource planning and shared accountability. In this sense, Chronos serves as a vital backbone. But the key lies in using this structure with flexibility, so it becomes a support system rather than a constraint.

The most effective schedules are not just mechanically filled. They reflect intention. Different times of day hold different energy. Some hours invite deep focus, while others are better suited for connection or rest. Honoring this natural rhythm adds depth to planning. It creates space for Kairos - the unexpected but meaningful moments that can't be predicted or controlled. This balanced approach invites professionals to work with time rather than against it.

The relationship between deadlines and motivation is complex. When deadlines are self-directed or connected to personal values, they can inspire momentum. But when they are experienced as external pressure, they can lead to burnout or avoidance. Professionals may begin to feel trapped in a cycle of chasing deliverables, rather than engaging meaningfully with the work itself. Rethinking how we relate to these time markers allows for more sustainable motivation and a healthier pace.

Chronos also shapes how we think about progress. In many settings, success is defined by measurable markers. But not all growth moves in a straight line. Sometimes a pause leads to clarity. Sometimes a setback leads to innovation. When time is seen only as forward motion, we may miss the richness found in stillness or recalibration. Redefining progress to include both movement and meaning creates a more complete view of achievement.

Many modern tools - calendars, apps, time-tracking systems - are designed to maximize efficiency. They provide clarity but can also contribute to overload. When every minute is accounted for, the space for curiosity and creativity can shrink. This reveals a core insight: controlling time too tightly can diminish our ability to experience it fully. Making room for pauses, transitions, and spontaneous insight allows time to breathe and reconnects us to a more human pace.

Scheduling and deadlines also impact collaboration. Shared timelines create alignment, making it easier to coordinate across roles and teams. But strict linear frameworks can clash with differing work styles or cultural attitudes about time. Creating shared rhythms requires empathy and adaptability. Recognizing that people engage with time differently leads to healthier collaboration and stronger relationships.

Using Chronos well requires more than external control. It asks for internal clarity. Time management becomes a form of self-leadership - the ability to match discipline with presence, urgency with perspective. When deadlines are seen as tools for focus rather than pressure points, they invite growth. Professionals who move fluidly within Chronos while remaining open to change often discover more ease and effectiveness in their work.

Practical strategies matter too. Prioritizing work, setting boundaries, reviewing commitments regularly - these are not just time tactics. They are choices that support both output and well-being. Equally important is the willingness to adapt when life shifts. Schedules should hold structure, but they should also bend. Time is not a rigid grid. It is a living current, shaped by attention and intention.

Reframing scheduling and deadlines through the lens of Chronos allows for a deeper conversation about how we work. It reminds us that structure supports momentum, but it does not define the whole experience. When we pair Chronos with the sensitivity of Kairos, we bring both alignment and insight into our professional lives. This integration moves us beyond control into a rhythm that supports not only productivity, but meaning.

Challenges of Over-Emphasizing Chronos at Work

In many professional environments, time is viewed through a narrow lens of precision, punctuality, and deadlines. Chronos - the sequential, quantitative experience of time - dominates the way work is structured and how productivity is assessed. It offers order and predictability, two qualities essential to managing complexity in organizations. But when Chronos is overemphasized, it introduces a series of challenges that quietly undermine both individual well-being and collective effectiveness.

Rigid time structures can limit creativity. When tasks are expected to fit into preassigned time slots, professionals may feel pressured to produce on command rather than allowing insight to emerge naturally. This pressure can crowd out the mental space needed for exploration, reflection, or inspiration. Ideas often require room to breathe, yet in many workplaces, the demand for visible output leaves little tolerance for work that resists quantification. The unintended result is that systems designed for efficiency may block the very breakthroughs they are meant to encourage.

The pressure created by a Chronos-driven culture also takes a toll on mental well-being. Constant attention to deadlines and measurable output can foster chronic stress. The internal clock speeds up. The workday begins to feel like a race. When there is no room to pause or reflect, professionals may lose the ability to connect meaningfully with their work. The deeper purpose behind daily effort fades. Over time, this disconnect can lead to burnout - not simply from overwork, but from the feeling that time itself has become something to battle rather than engage with intentionally.

Time pressure also reshapes how people relate to one another. In tightly scheduled environments, meetings become condensed, conversations are streamlined, and decisions are made with speed in mind. While efficiency improves, the cost is often depth. Rich dialogue gives way to transaction. Opportunities for trust, insight, or genuine connection are lost in the rush to keep things moving. Even teams with well-organized calendars may struggle to adapt or innovate if interpersonal dynamics are treated as secondary to timelines.

Strict adherence to Chronos also reduces adaptability. Organizations today must respond to shifting conditions, emerging challenges, and unexpected opportunities. These moments rarely fit neatly into a schedule. A system built too tightly around fixed timelines may discourage experimentation or risk-taking. In such environments, professionals become reactive - executing tasks efficiently, but overlooking inflection points that could shift the course of a project or spark meaningful change. Kairos - the felt sense of the right time - often slips by unnoticed when every moment has already been assigned.

A fixation on the clock also fragments attention. Juggling overlapping deadlines and multitasking through tightly packed schedules pulls professionals away from the present moment. Focus becomes diluted. The mind hovers between what just happened and what needs to happen next. This division not only affects performance but also limits learning and presence. When time becomes something to conquer, it is difficult to be truly engaged with the task at hand.

There's a cost to quality as well. When time is treated only as a unit to manage, work is often reduced to checklists and completion metrics. Depth and craftsmanship may suffer. Projects become about finishing quickly rather than thinking deeply. For individuals, this leads to a diminished sense of purpose. For organizations, it can mean missed opportunities to create lasting value. Professional growth often requires reflection, iteration, and patience - qualities that are difficult to honor when the primary goal is speed.

In people-focused roles such as leadership or counseling, over-reliance on Chronos weakens relational depth. Human dynamics are not linear. Empathy, emotional intelligence, and intuition emerge in moments that are not bound by the clock. Leaders who are constantly moving from one scheduled task to the next may miss subtle cues - changes in mood, unspoken concerns, or chances to offer timely support. Over time, this lack of attunement erodes trust and makes it harder to lead with authenticity.

Chronos-based scheduling also impacts learning and development. Professional growth is often treated as a structured process with clear timelines and deliverables. But deep learning rarely conforms to a strict schedule. When training becomes another task to complete, curiosity gives way to compliance. Professionals may meet development goals on paper but miss the chance to integrate knowledge meaningfully. Growth becomes superficial. Over time, this undermines both individual advancement and organizational innovation.

Rest is another area affected by an overemphasis on measured time. Breaks are often scheduled - slotted between meetings or justified as productivity strategies - but the deeper purpose of rest is often overlooked. Downtime allows the brain to reset. It gives space for insight and creativity to reemerge. When every moment is packed, rest becomes one more thing to manage, rather than a source of renewal. Without periods of quiet and disengagement, the quality of attention and the capacity to sustain performance begin to diminish.

Chronos also plays a subtle role in shaping workplace culture. Environments that elevate speed and measurement may favor certain time orientations over others. People who thrive under pressure or who work quickly are often celebrated, while those who process more slowly or need reflection time may feel sidelined. This dynamic can narrow inclusivity and reduce the range of voices that shape decisions. Recognizing the diverse ways people relate to time opens up more thoughtful and equitable ways to structure work.

While punctuality, scheduling, and structure are necessary, they should not be the only standards by which time is measured or valued. Too often, the systems designed to bring clarity end up reducing the richness of the work experience. If time is seen only as a currency to be spent efficiently, then its potential to support growth, creativity, and meaning is lost.

The risks of over-investing in Chronos remind us that time should not be a force we simply endure. It should be something we engage with intentionally. When professionals learn to balance the structure of clock time with awareness of moments that invite presence, creativity, or connection, they move closer to a fuller experience of time. Chronos can support clarity. But it must be balanced with the awareness that not everything valuable fits into a schedule.

A mature relationship with time integrates both the measurable and the meaningful. It allows deadlines to serve progress without becoming the sole markers of success. It leaves space for Kairos - those moments that invite intuition, insight, or change. By cultivating this awareness, professionals move from managing time to working with it - not just meeting expectations, but shaping experiences that support deep, sustainable engagement.

Chapter 7: Using Kairos for Creative Breakthroughs

Unlocking the power of Kairos begins with learning to sense those fleeting windows where something more becomes possible. These are the moments when timing, readiness, and clarity come together - not through planning or pressure, but through presence. They can't be scheduled. They don't respond to force. But they can be noticed, and when acted on, they often change everything.

In creative work, true breakthroughs rarely arrive through constant effort alone. They emerge when the mind is both engaged and open, when there is enough stillness to recognize a new angle or a subtle shift. The creative process requires discipline, but it also requires space - the space to notice when the right idea begins to form, when a new direction quietly presents itself. Kairos lives in that space. It does not call for more hours. It calls for deeper attention.

This chapter invites a different posture toward creativity - one grounded in patience and presence. Rather than pushing harder, it's about listening more closely. It's about cultivating an internal sensitivity to the rhythms of your work, so that insight feels less like a surprise and more like a natural response. When you begin to sense when something is ready - when the energy shifts, when an idea begins to open - that is Kairos making itself known.

Spotting these moments requires stillness and speed. Stillness to recognize them. Speed to move with them. Acting at the right time means staying close to your own experience, trusting intuition, and being willing to shift direction when something important surfaces. This responsiveness doesn't replace discipline. It refines it. It makes the work not only more alive, but more aligned.

Kairos brings a kind of energy that renews. When a solution emerges in its own time, when a breakthrough appears without being forced, the result often feels more than efficient - it feels true. These moments elevate the work beyond output. They create momentum that is both creative and sustainable. They support a way of working that honors both structure and flow.

Learning to recognize Kairos is not about waiting passively. It's about preparing actively - creating the mental and emotional space where timing can be felt and trusted. In doing so, creativity shifts from something to chase to something to respond to. And in that shift, new possibilities open, not just for what gets created, but for how it feels to create.

Identifying Creative Kairos Opportunities

In the ongoing journey of creative work, learning to recognize the presence of Kairos becomes essential. These moments rarely arrive with clear signals. More often, they show up quietly - tucked inside a shift in energy, a conversation that takes an unexpected turn, or a fleeting moment of clarity in the middle of something routine. Yet within these subtle openings lives the potential for breakthrough, insight, and meaningful change.

Kairos asks for a different kind of attention. It can't be scheduled or summoned. It must be noticed. Unlike Chronos, which operates on the surface through structure and sequence, Kairos moves beneath - emerging when internal readiness meets external conditions in just the right way. It doesn't demand speed. It asks for awareness.

Recognizing Kairos begins with tuning in to the rhythms of your inner world. Sometimes it feels like a sudden alignment - an idea that takes shape in response to something indirect, or a burst of clarity that cuts through a period of uncertainty. Other times, it comes with emotional intensity or a quiet sense of urgency. These signals are not loud, but they are consistent. The more you learn to listen, the more familiar they become.

Kairos is also shaped by the world around you. Disruptions in routine, conversations that shift perspective, or unexpected patterns in your environment can all create conditions where Kairos becomes visible. The key is not just to notice the moment, but to recognize when it intersects with your own readiness - your preparation, your energy, and your willingness to act.

Not every opportunity is Kairos. Distraction can mimic possibility. Urgency can masquerade as inspiration. What distinguishes a Kairos moment is convergence - a harmony of timing, skill, and insight. When the elements align, there is a quiet clarity that invites focused movement rather than reaction.

This is where creativity and Kairos meet. Creative energy needs space. It thrives when it is allowed to flow, not forced into tight containers. But without Kairos, even open space can become scattered. Kairos offers direction - a current that gathers your energy and points it toward what matters most. It's not about doing more. It's about acting when the time is right.

To develop sensitivity to Kairos, reflection is essential. Journaling unexpected insights, shifts in momentum, or periods of creative engagement can reveal patterns over time. These reflections build awareness. They help you recognize not only what the moment felt like, but how you responded. Over time, this becomes a kind of map - one that orients you toward Kairos more reliably.

Flow is another indicator. When time feels like it's dissolving, and attention deepens naturally, it often signals that Kairos is present. Flow is a form of alignment - where skill, interest, and context come together. While it cannot be forced, it can be invited. Creating the conditions for flow - through space, presence, and intention - increases your chances of stepping into Kairos when it arrives.

Importantly, Kairos is not always neat. It can show up in ambiguity, in periods that feel unclear or chaotic. Recognizing Kairos in these moments requires trust - not in the outcome, but in the unfolding process. It means letting go of rigid timelines and learning to respond to what is real in the moment, even if it doesn't yet make perfect sense.

Preparation matters here. While Kairos cannot be manufactured, it can be welcomed. Building in unstructured time, shifting creative environments, or allowing space for experimentation helps cultivate a state of openness. You're not forcing inspiration. You're creating space for it to land.

Technology, when used intentionally, can support this awareness. Setting reminders to pause or reflect, capturing fleeting thoughts before they disappear, or building digital spaces for ideas to grow can help ensure Kairos is not missed. The goal is not to chase moments but to be ready when they appear.

Professional environments add a layer of complexity. Deadlines, meetings, and schedules tend to favor Chronos. But Kairos can still thrive here - if there is a dual awareness. The most effective professionals and leaders learn to operate within structure while remaining alert to moments that call for change. They know when to follow the plan and when to break from it.

History offers countless examples. Creative breakthroughs, scientific discoveries, and transformative decisions are rarely the result of effort alone. They happen when individuals recognize a moment - and respond to it fully. These are Kairos moments. And they remind us that timing, not just effort, shapes outcomes.

In the end, identifying Kairos is about building a different relationship with time. It's not just about getting things done. It's about learning when to move, when to wait, and when to step outside the schedule to follow something deeper. This awareness allows you to align effort with timing - turning ordinary moments into extraordinary ones.

By cultivating this sensitivity, you build a compass that guides you not through rigidity, but through rhythm. You no longer chase every opportunity. You learn to recognize the ones that matter. And in doing so, you shift from simply producing work to creating work that resonates - not only with others, but with yourself.

Case Studies of Kairos in Artistic and Innovative Work

When we think about moments of breakthrough in art, science, or innovation, it's easy to focus on talent, technique, or sheer persistence. These are the visible drivers, the ones we can measure and name. But underneath them often lies something more elusive - Kairos. The opportune moment. The intersection where preparation, intuition, and timing align just enough to make something new possible. It's not the march of the clock that shapes these turning points. It's the quiet shift - often brief, always meaningful - that opens a door and invites us to step through.

Consider the filmmaker who, after years of working within familiar formulas, captured something extraordinary not through a high-budget production, but through an unplanned shoot where everything fell into place. The light was right. The actors' energy clicked. The story came alive in a way no rehearsal could script. That moment wasn't scheduled. It wasn't controlled. It was recognized and embraced. And that decision - to trust the moment - transformed the work and gave it a lasting voice. This is the essence of Kairos in action.

In music, similar moments shape the arc of creative lives. One pianist, known for a disciplined, almost mathematical approach to practice, found new inspiration after an unexpected, improvised collaboration. The encounter invited a different rhythm - less structured, more alive - and sparked a body of work that moved far beyond technical mastery. The pianist didn't plan the moment. But when it appeared, they were ready. And that readiness made all the difference.

Kairos is just as present in collaborative settings. In one design studio, a stalled product led to a spontaneous brainstorming session that veered off course. What emerged was an idea initially dismissed as too soft, too unconventional. But something about the moment made it stick. The right people were in the room. The energy shifted. A junior designer spoke up. That pivot - small and unplanned - redefined the project. It's a reminder that Kairos doesn't always announce itself loudly. Sometimes it arrives as a subtle nudge, and only later do we recognize its significance.

Even in physically expressive forms like dance, Kairos shows up. A choreographer once shared how a storm cancelled rehearsals and forced the company to improvise without structure. That disruption became the breakthrough. In letting go of the planned performance, the dancers rediscovered their own vocabulary. The final piece was shaped not by choreography, but by what emerged in the pause. Critics later praised its originality, but its source was simple: the decision to embrace what the moment allowed.

Painters, too, speak of Kairos in deeply personal ways. One described a moment when a sudden shift in light transformed an entire scene. The decision to change direction - to follow what was happening rather than what had been planned - altered the work and, eventually, the course of their style. These shifts are not about waiting passively for inspiration. They are about noticing - and choosing - when something more is available.

Writers often meet Kairos in the quiet tension between effort and surrender. A novelist, after months of stalled progress, once described a single evening when a new voice emerged in their manuscript - unforced, unfamiliar, and completely right. That shift didn't come from trying harder. It came from listening more closely and being willing to let go of what wasn't working. The novel that followed connected with readers in ways earlier drafts never had. It wasn't just better writing. It was the right writing - born from the right time.

Kairos also plays out at larger scales. The rise of abstract expressionism didn't happen in isolation. It emerged when artists began responding to the emotional undercurrents of their time - postwar tension, shifting cultural values, new questions about identity and meaning. The work broke with tradition not out of rebellion alone, but because something had shifted in the moment. The artists felt it. They named it through brushstrokes and form. And history changed course.

Scientific breakthroughs carry the same texture. The invention of the laser, for instance, wasn't a straight line. It came through a series of unrelated experiments and unexpected insights that converged at the right time. The scientists involved were prepared - technically and intellectually - but it was their attunement to timing that allowed them to act. Kairos was present, and they recognized it.

These stories - across fields and eras - remind us that Kairos is not a passive force. It asks for participation. It asks us to stay close enough to our work to sense when something is shifting, even if we don't yet know what it means. It asks for trust - in ourselves, in our process, in the unfolding nature of time.

What we learn from these moments is that preparation matters. Skill matters. But neither can replace the quiet power of right timing. When professionals become too attached to schedules or outcomes, they risk missing the subtle signals that Kairos offers. Conversely, those who remain open - who leave room for the unexpected, who make space for emergence - often find themselves on the edge of something new.

Practicing this awareness doesn't require abandoning structure. It requires softening it. Leaving space in the day. Listening more closely to when energy shifts. Noticing when something in the air feels different. These practices - small, consistent, intentional - help create the internal conditions where Kairos is more likely to be recognized and more easily followed.

At its heart, Kairos is a teacher. It invites us to move beyond rigid thinking and into a deeper relationship with time itself. One where we don't just plan and produce, but also respond and receive. In doing so, we allow creativity to become what it is meant to be - not just output, but expression. Not just efficiency, but resonance.

Kairos moments feel fleeting, but their impact can be lasting. They don't just change what we make. They change how we see. They connect us to something larger than the task at hand - a timing that lives between structure and spontaneity. Those who learn to sense this timing shape their work in ways that can't be duplicated. They don't just keep time. They move with it.

Chapter 8: Balancing Chronos & Kairos in Decisions

When it comes to making meaningful decisions, the real challenge often lies in holding two very different kinds of time at once. Chronos gives us structure. It keeps the trains running, the meetings scheduled, the work tracked. It's the time of planners, clocks, and carefully organized calendars. But alongside it runs another current - Kairos - the subtle rhythm of timing that can't be measured or forced. It's the felt sense of "now," when something clicks into place and the path forward becomes clear.

Too often, decisions are rushed to meet external demands without listening for the right internal signal. We become locked into schedules, responding reflexively rather than intentionally. But some of the most effective choices - the ones that change direction or unlock new energy - don't emerge from pressure. They emerge from presence. They happen when we pause long enough to notice what is actually unfolding, both within and around us.

This is where the dance between Chronos and Kairos matters most. It's not about choosing one over the other. It's about learning when to follow structure and when to listen for something deeper. When we bring attention to both dimensions, decision-making shifts. It becomes less about reacting to timelines and more about aligning with timing - the kind that brings clarity, momentum, and meaning.

Trusting this process requires practice. It means respecting the discipline of Chronos without letting it dominate. It also means developing the confidence to wait for Kairos - to allow intuition, context, and readiness to shape the moment of action. This kind of discernment doesn't always follow logic, but it often leads to better outcomes. It asks not just what needs to be done, but when and how it should happen.

Professionals and creatives who develop this dual awareness often describe feeling more grounded in their choices. They are still productive, still responsive, but they move with a different quality - one marked by timing rather than urgency. Their decisions don't just check boxes. They carry weight. They create movement that feels both deliberate and alive.

This integration is what turns decision-making into something more than task management. It becomes a craft - an ongoing practice of sensing, balancing, and responding. When we learn to trust both the clock and the moment, we find our way toward decisions that not only meet the demands of now, but also open the door to what's next.

Strategies to Integrate Quantitative and Qualitative Time

In the journey toward balancing Chronos and Kairos, one of the most crucial challenges is learning to weave together quantitative and qualitative experiences of time. Quantitative time, represented by Chronos, is measurable, segmented, and predictable. On the other hand, qualitative time embodied by Kairos is experiential, intuitive, and often defies clocks and calendars. These two dimensions may seem at odds, yet their integration is essential for richer decision-making and living a fuller life.

Think about your daily routines. Most of what you do is scheduled by the ticking of the clock: meetings, deadlines, appointments. This is your Chronos world, where time is sliced into discrete units that help organize your life. But within this structure, the most transformative moments might arrive spontaneously - a sudden insight, a perfect moment to speak, or an opportunity that opens unexpectedly. These Kairos moments are qualitative experiences, existing outside the rigidity of measured time.

To integrate these divergent experiences effectively, we first need to acknowledge that time is not just a neutral container for activities. It is a fluid, multi-dimensional phenomenon. Chronos might set the frame, but Kairos fills the frame with meaning. When making decisions, balancing these two means more than watching the clock and checking a calendar; it requires cultivating sensitivity to when something significant is poised to happen.

So how do you cultivate this sensitivity? One foundational strategy is intentional presence within your Chronos schedule. This means designing space - not just for task completion but for moments of reflection and openness. Many fall into the trap of overloading their quantitative schedules, often mistaking fullness of activity for productivity or success. In doing so, they miss Kairos impulses that don't fit neatly into rigid plans. Effective integration means allowing your schedule to breathe, carving out unstructured time that invites Kairos to show up.

Consider this: when you're in back-to-back meetings or rushing between commitments, opportunities for Kairos - those crucial, timely moments of insight or connection - are easily drowned out. By setting aside blocks of flexible time, you create a period where spontaneous alignment with deeper insights becomes possible. These intervals act as a bridge between Chronos and Kairos, affording the mental and emotional space needed for qualitative time to unfold.

Another strategy involves developing heightened awareness and attunement to patterns beyond the second hand on the clock. This requires practicing mindfulness and reflective observation in your daily life. As you become more conscious of your internal rhythms and external cues, your ability to sense Kairos moments sharpens. This internal tuning blends the quantitative cues of Chronos with the qualitative signals of Kairos, steering you toward optimal moments for decisions that matter.

Technology, when used mindfully, can serve as a valuable ally in this integration. For example, calendar apps and task lists keep Chronos organized, but it's vital to resist letting technology dictate every beat of your day. Instead, use reminders and alerts to highlight not just deadlines but also moments to pause and check in with how you're feeling or whether new opportunities have presented themselves. In this way, your tools support both dimensions without becoming enslaving.

Furthermore, storytelling and narrative thinking can help bridge the immeasurable world of Kairos with the measurable realm of Chronos. When reviewing your day or preparing for decisions, frame your experiences not only in terms of what time you spent but also in how significant or transformative those moments were. This reflection allows you to internalize lessons from both quantitative tracking and qualitative meaning, leading to wiser, more holistic choices in the future.

Decision-making frameworks can explicitly incorporate criteria that honor both Chronos and Kairos. Instead of focusing purely on efficiency or cost-benefit analyses, integrate measures that account for timing readiness, intuitive alignment, and emotional resonance. For instance, when evaluating a project or opportunity, consider not only the deadlines and resource allocations but also the flow of enthusiasm, the quality of engagement, and whether the timing feels inherently right. These softer, qualitative aspects often hint at Kairos moments that can dramatically influence outcomes.

Importantly, embracing uncertainty as an ally rather than an enemy enhances this integration. Chronos thrives on certainty - fixed schedules, linear progress, clear endpoints. Kairos dances in uncertainty, calling for trust in intuition and timing beyond the obvious. By shifting your mindset to allow room for ambiguity and unknown possibility within your structured time, you lean into the flow where Kairos operates. This doesn't mean abandoning deadlines, but rather layering flexibility and openness into how you meet them. Such an approach enriches decision-making with both data and insight.

Collaboration also benefits from blending quantitative and qualitative time perspectives. Workplaces often emphasize punctuality and task completion, yet breakthrough ideas frequently emerge from unplanned dialogue and spontaneous exchanges. Encouraging teams to balance scheduled work with spaces for open-ended interaction sparks creativity and responsiveness. It's a way to institutionalize the interplay of Chronos and Kairos, making room for both structure and serendipity to coexist productively.

In personal growth, integrating Chronos and Kairos means recognizing that timing is integral to readiness. You might schedule time for learning or reflection, which honors Chronos, but true transformation often happens in Kairos-infused moments - when a sudden realization or an emotional breakthrough arises unexpectedly. Preparing for such moments requires commitment to long-term habits while remaining agile enough to pivot when intuitions from Kairos point the way. This balance leads to growth that's both disciplined and inspired.

Practically speaking, journaling can be a powerful tool in this integration process. Keeping track of not just what you do, but how and when you do it, helps you identify recurring Kairos moments intertwined with your Chronos schedule. Writing about experiences in terms of energy, flow, and timing fosters deeper understanding of how these dimensions of time interact uniquely for you. Over weeks and months, this practice uncovers insightful patterns that can inform future decision-making, helping you to trust your timing instincts in tandem with logical scheduling.

At its heart, integrating quantitative and qualitative time is a matter of becoming fluent in two languages of time - and learning when to listen to each one. Chronos provides the grammar and structure needed to navigate life practically. Kairos offers the poetry and meaning that transform simple moments into milestones. When balanced, these forms of temporal intelligence create a powerful synergy, allowing you to act with both precision and purpose.

The subtle art lies in cultivating patience for Kairos to arrive, without losing momentum in your Chronos commitments. This may look like setting goals with timelines flexible enough to shift as insights guide, or approaching deadlines with a mindset open to new information and opportunities. Your decisions gain depth when informed both by the logical constraints of measured time and the intuitive urgency of timely moments.

Ultimately, the integration encourages a rhythm of living that respects the clock without being ruled by it. It values punctuality yet embraces mystery, structure yet welcomes spontaneity. This dynamic balance fosters an empowered experience of time - not as a tyrant stamping on your days, but as an ally inviting you to dance fully in each moment.

In practice, every decision becomes an opportunity to blend what can be scheduled and planned with what must be felt and seized. Whether steering a career, nurturing relationships, or embarking on creative projects, weaving Chronos and Kairos together enriches the quality of what you accomplish and deepens your connection to time itself.

By embedding these strategies within your approach to time, you transform time management from a mechanical process to a living art - a skill that integrates measurement and meaning seamlessly. The result is a richer, more responsive engagement with life's flow, inviting you to become not just a keeper of time, but its masterful participant.

Overcoming Bias Toward Chronos-Only Perspectives

Living in a world dominated by clocks, calendars, and precise schedules, it's easy to fall into the trap of valuing only the measurable aspect of time, Chronos. From early schooling to corporate culture, our systems reward punctuality, deadlines, and linear progress. This emphasis skews our perception, making us overlook the equally critical, yet less tangible, dimension of time often referred to as Kairos - the opportune moment. Overcoming the ingrained bias toward Chronos-only thinking is essential to achieving a more balanced, richer experience of time, both personally and professionally.

That bias isn't accidental. The very structure of most societies depends on Chronos. Industries, governments, and educational institutions thrive on it because it provides order and predictability. It's what most people associate with productivity and success. The bias develops subtly, shaping our view that time only "counts" when it's quantifiable - when tasks get checked off a list, when hours translate to bills, or when one can measure progress by minutes ticking away. This is a powerful conditioning that influences how firmly we hold onto routines, how rigidly we stick to calendars, and how we prioritize one activity over another.

Yet, this rigid attachment stifles more than just creativity; it limits our awareness of Kairos - the moments pregnant with potential, timing that transcends the linear flow of clocks. Kairos invites us to listen beyond deadlines and schedules, to notice when an idea is ripening or when a situation is ripe for change. It's the subtle sense that signals when to act or hold back, something that can't be quantified with precision. The challenge lies in our cultural conditioning, which often dismisses or overlooks these qualitative moments as unproductive or irrelevant.

Recognizing and challenging this bias begins with cultivating awareness. Notice how often your decisions rely purely on Chronos. Which goals get prioritized because they have a deadline, and which get neglected because they don't fit neatly on a calendar? In meetings, how frequently do you focus on staying on schedule rather than assessing the flow of ideas or the pulse of the group's energy? These questions might reveal how embedded Chronos-only thinking has become in your habits. Awareness here is the first crack in the wall, opening a door for Kairos to enter.

There's also an emotional component to consider. Chronos-oriented thinking tends to create a sense of urgency - and sometimes anxiety - that can cloud judgment. Deadlines loom, hours slip, and the pressure to accomplish tasks becomes relentless. While urgency has its place, it often obscures deeper wisdom that Kairos moments offer: the right timing for meaningful conversations, the spark of creative insight, or even the pause that allows better decision making. Letting go of the idea that everything must be done on time creates space for intuition, sensitivity, and openness to emerge.

At its core, overcoming this bias means appreciating that time is not only a sequence of increments but also a landscape of moments charged with potential. This shift requires moving beyond linear thinking to embrace a more holistic view that values timing's qualitative nuances. It means trusting the rhythms of life that can't be scheduled on a planner and honoring the pauses and flows that defy the clock's tyranny.

Integrating Kairos into daily life doesn't mean abandoning Chronos but rebalancing it. One practical way of escaping Chronos-only traps is to build intentional breaks into rigid schedules. These moments become opportunities to reflect, observe, and sense what Kairos might be signaling. Even a short pause can reveal insights that a relentless march of to-dos would never uncover. This small act of deliberately stepping away from linear time invites creativity, intuition, and better judgment - all vital for effective decision making.

Another key is questioning the cultural narratives we internalize about time and productivity. We often equate busy schedules with success or worth, but embracing Kairos challenges this premise. Sometimes, the most valuable use of time isn't about how much you do but about when and how you act. Kairos teaches us that timing can outweigh the quantity of effort. Learning to listen for those moments that feel right allows us to align our actions with deeper currents of opportunity rather than merely race against the clock.

Shifting from a Chronos-dominated mindset to a balanced one also requires developing trust - trust in the process, trust in one's intuition, and trust in the unfolding of events outside strict schedules. This often involves vulnerability because letting go of rigid timelines can feel risky or countercultural at first. However, when people allow themselves to sense Kairos, they discover a richer texture of experiences and often better outcomes. For instance, decisions made by tuning into timely inspiration rather than strictly following deadlines often prove more creative, effective, and fulfilling.

This balance is particularly crucial for professionals and creatives alike. Those who produce innovative work or navigate complex human interactions often face a tension between deliverables paced by Chronos and moments of insight heralded by Kairos. Overcoming Chronos bias helps these individuals avoid burnout and mechanical routine. Instead, they unlock intuitive wisdom and creative breakthroughs by embracing opportune moments. This doesn't contradict planning but rather enriches it, turning time management from a rigid chore into a dynamic dance with opportunity.

It's also helpful to surround ourselves with environments that support Kairos as much as Chronos. Organizations and teams that insist on relentless scheduling without room for emergent moments can inadvertently suppress creativity and adaptability. Leaders who recognize the value of both dimensions foster cultures where timing and intuition are welcomed alongside efficiency and deadlines. This creates not just better decision-making outcomes but healthier, more engaged people who feel trusted to harness both quantitative and qualitative time.

While overcoming the bias toward Chronos-only perspectives may feel like an uphill battle against a deeply entrenched cultural norm, it's a necessary evolution for those seeking a more vibrant and meaningful engagement with time. It invites an awakening to the subtleties beneath the seconds and minutes - that edge where inspiration, readiness, and action converge. Embracing this fuller picture leads to choices made not just with the clock's tick but with the heart's knowing.

The journey to rebalance Chronos and Kairos asks us to loosen our grip on measurement as the sole marker of value. It's about creating mental space where intuition and signs can emerge clearly within the rhythm of daily life. The payoff goes beyond improved productivity; it is a deeper alignment with life's flow, where purpose, timing, and action find harmony. This transformation isn't simply strategic - it is liberating. Those who master this dance move beyond the constraints of the clock and step confidently into the richest potential moments life offers.

Ultimately, overcoming the Chronos-only bias empowers us to live not just through time but with it, embracing the intersections of measured progression and fleeting opportunity. This balanced perspective unlocks a fuller experience of time's gifts - realizing that success, fulfillment, and wisdom don't merely happen on schedule but often in the spaces between.

Chapter 9: Mastering Chronos to Build Focus

Harnessing Chronos, the relentless forward tick of measurable time, is not about becoming a rigid automaton chained to the clock. It is about cultivating a disciplined rhythm that sharpens focus and fuels meaningful progress. By intentionally aligning our daily actions with Chronos's steady cadence, we tap into a powerful framework that transforms scattered intentions into purposeful momentum - allowing space for growth without suffocation.

When we master Chronos, we create structure that doesn't just dictate our hours. It empowers us to dive deeper into tasks with clarity and resolve, fostering habits that reinforce productivity while preserving enough flexibility for the unexpected. This mastery becomes the gateway to turning time from a passive measurement into an active ally. In doing so, we open doors to sustained achievement and a more centered, focused life.

Tools and Techniques to Harness Chronos Effectively

In today's fast-paced world, mastering Chronos - the sequential, measurable time - requires more than just watching the clock. It demands strategic tools and practical techniques that help us tap into time's linear flow and turn it into a powerful ally for discipline and focus. Whether you're a professional juggling multiple deadlines, a creative seeking consistent productivity, or a lifelong learner striving for meaningful progress, understanding how to harness Chronos effectively is key to building a sustainable routine without feeling overwhelmed.

One of the essential tools to engage with Chronos effectively is deliberate scheduling. Unlike reactive planning, where tasks pile up unpredictably, proactive scheduling helps frame your day with intention. By carving out distinct blocks of time designated for specific activities, you create a rhythm that respects Chronos's steady pulse. This technique does more than organize - it trains your mind to anticipate work, rest, and creative flow in sequence. It breaks down complex projects into manageable segments, making progress tangible rather than abstract.

Yet, scheduling alone isn't enough. It's equally important to adopt tools that keep you aware and aligned with Chronos without triggering burnout. Techniques like the Pomodoro Method, which involves focused work intervals followed by short breaks, mirror natural attention spans and biological rhythms. This method leverages Chronos by anchoring effort within fixed timeframes, creating a sense of urgency balanced by regular rest. Many find that this cyclical approach sharpens concentration and curbs procrastination, fostering a disciplined engagement with time's linear passage.

Technology offers numerous solutions to help track and optimize Chronos. Time-tracking apps serve as mirrors showing how you actually spend each minute, exposing hidden pockets of wasted time or distractions. When used mindfully, these tools don't just monitor - they cultivate accountability. Seeing the data visually can inspire behavioral shifts, pushing you to more conscious time investment. Yet, caution is needed: relying solely on digital timers and notifications can fragment focus if overused or poorly managed. The goal is to use technology as a subtle nudge, not an intrusive taskmaster.

Another foundational technique centers on prioritization strategies like the Eisenhower Matrix or the Pareto Principle. These methods help distinguish tasks that deserve your Chronos investment from those that dilute your efforts. By categorizing activities by urgency and importance, you align your time with purpose rather than reaction. Distilling your to-dos to a meaningful core not only preserves mental clarity - it also builds endurance. This ensures Chronos is not wasted chasing irrelevant deadlines or trivial distractions, but instead powers what truly moves you forward.

Discipline and focus flourish in environments that signal intentional time use. Creating physical or mental spaces dedicated to Chronos-focused work reinforces routine and minimizes interruptions. Even simple actions - like setting a consistent start time, clearing clutter, or wearing specific attire - can anchor your brain in a productive state. These rituals act as extrinsic cues tied to Chronos, conditioning your body and mind to respond reliably. With repetition, such cues transition from conscious effort to subconscious triggers, making disciplined engagement a habit rather than a chore.

Perhaps less obvious but equally impactful is mastering the art of micro-deadlines. Breaking tasks into smaller, time-bound checkpoints generates a steady flow of momentum that capitalizes on Chronos's measurable nature. Instead of waiting for a distant deadline to loom, these mini-goals create multiple moments of accomplishment. Each fulfilled checkpoint releases dopamine, reinforcing focus and motivation. This technique counteracts the tendency to delay and procrastinate, embedding a forward-moving pulse into even the most complex or daunting projects.

Moreover, learning to track personal energy cycles is a subtle yet profound tool for syncing with Chronos. Everyone naturally experiences highs and lows of alertness throughout the day, and when your activities align with these ebbs and flows, Chronos turns into a servant rather than a taskmaster. For instance, scheduling demanding tasks during peak energy periods and reserving more routine work for slower phases amplifies efficiency. Awareness of these internal rhythms - minute to minute and hour to hour - adds a layer of depth to time management that calendars alone can't provide.

Alongside these practical techniques exists the powerful mental practice of time framing. This involves consciously viewing segments of Chronos with an attitude of respect and purpose, rather than obligation or anxiety. Time framing shifts your perception from "I have to finish this by 5 PM" to "I have 3 focused hours to create something meaningful." Such reframing engenders autonomy and engagement. It makes Chronos a container for intentional action instead of a ticking clock of stress, subtly transforming the experience of time from resistance to flow.

It's also necessary to cultivate a mindful relationship with time through reflection and adjustment. Chronos mastery isn't about rigid adherence to a plan but about iterative refinement. Taking moments at the end of days or weeks to analyze how well your strategies align with your natural rhythms and goals opens pathways to ongoing improvement. This reflective tool guards against stagnation and frustration by embracing flexibility within discipline. It's the dance between consistency and responsiveness, where Chronos becomes both guide and collaborator rather than an adversary.

Humility in the face of Chronos is a hidden but critical technique. Accepting that some things are simply outside your control - unexpected interruptions, fluctuating workload, or surprise opportunities - cultivates resilience. When you can bend without breaking, Chronos no longer feels like an inflexible master but a fellow traveler. This mindset encourages you to keep focus steady and discipline intact, even when time's linear flow seems disrupted. Paradoxically, this acceptance often leads to heightened efficiency and calm, because it frees you from futile resistance.

Group accountability frameworks also harness Chronos's power by creating external drivers to maintain discipline. Whether through peer partnerships, professional coaching, or mastermind groups, shared timelines increase commitment. The social dimension adds a layer where Chronos is not just personal but communal, mobilizing collective energy toward timely progress. This relational technique often injects motivation when internal reserves wane, reminding us that our experience of time is both individual and interconnected.

Finally, one cannot underestimate the transformative role of purpose when engaging with Chronos. Tools and techniques matter most when embedded in a clear, compelling why. When every unit of time is tethered to your broader mission or values, even the most mundane schedules take on significance. Discipline becomes meaningful rather than mechanical, focus becomes inspired rather than forced. In this light, Chronos moves from a relentless measurer of moments to a co-creator of a life lived intentionally and fully.

Harnessing Chronos effectively is not about conquering time but conversing with it. Through an array of tools - scheduling, prioritization, energy alignment, micro-deadlines, reflection, and more - we refine our ability to channel the steady river of moments into a purposeful stream. This mastery builds a foundation for productivity that doesn't sacrifice creativity or wellbeing. It opens space for deeper focus and sustained discipline, creating a rhythmic harmony between ourselves and the linear flow of time that governs our lives.

Creating Sustainable Routines without Stifling Flexibility

In the quest to master Chronos, the ticking clock that governs our schedules and productivity, the challenge isn't merely about imposing discipline. It's about creating rhythms that sustain momentum without turning life into a rigid, mechanized grind. Sustainable routines serve as a framework, a skeleton on which the rich muscle of creativity and spontaneity can still thrive. Too often, people mistake routine for restriction. But when constructed thoughtfully, routines become the fertile soil from which consistent focus and energy grow.

What does it mean to craft routines that are, in a word, sustainable? It means they must be realistic - designed not for an idealized "perfect" self but for the person navigating real days, fluctuating motivation, unexpected demands, and the natural ebb and flow of mental and physical energy. When routines demand perfection or become too inflexible, they often crumble under pressure, leading to frustration and burnout. On the other hand, routines that acknowledge human variability allow room for adjustment, fostering a cycle of progress rather than paralysis.

Consider how a mathematical formula is rigid - plug in values, get a specific outcome. A sustainable routine, conversely, is more like a living organism. It responds and adapts to changes in environment and internal states. This doesn't mean abandoning the discipline that Chronos requires; it means respecting the natural rhythms that govern us. For professionals and creatives alike, this nuanced balance between consistency and adaptability is key to preserving both high performance and well-being.

One subtle but powerful principle in building such routines is to approach them as hypotheses rather than commandments. When you start a new routine, instead of vowing to adhere unbreakably, treat it as an experiment. Observe what works and what doesn't. Notice how certain timings align better with your focus, energy, or emotional state. When a routine proves draining or impractical, allow yourself to tinker with it rather than forcing adherence.

Humans aren't machines designed for constant output; we're dynamic beings operating within broader life contexts. Weekly meetings, family events, personal interests - all influence the energy and attention we can bring to disciplined pursuits. Incorporating flexibility means integrating these external variables thoughtfully. For instance, a routine might include a time-blocked schedule for deep work, but also carve out buffer periods to accommodate life's unpredictability or spontaneous inspiration.

The awareness that rigidity often kills productivity is rooted in biology as much as psychology. The brain thrives on certain patterns, to be sure, but it also needs novelty and recovery. This is why routines that incorporate breaks, variation, and moments of low-demand activity not only support sustained effort but enhance creativity and problem-solving. These "breathers" are not wasted time but essential regenerative spaces that keep the mind calibrated and ready for focused action.

Flexibility within routines acknowledges the dual nature of Chronos: the measurable, sequential time that demands structure - and the lived experience of time that requires flow. This duality invites us to build routines that hold firm in essentials yet remain fluid in delivery. For example, the essence of a morning routine might be to center yourself and prepare for the day ahead. How that looks - whether it's meditation, journaling, movement, or some other practice - can vary day to day based on how you're feeling or what your schedule demands.

Another critical aspect is psychological ownership. When people create routines that feel imposed from outside - whether by external deadlines, managers, or social expectations - they often resist or rebel against them. Sustainable routines emerge from aligned intention: they connect with your values and long-term aspirations, making discipline less of a chore and more of a meaningful commitment. When a routine ties into what truly matters, compliance turns into embrace.

It's also worth highlighting the importance of incremental progress. Building sustainable routines doesn't mean sudden, sweeping overhauls of your entire day. It's far more effective and empowering to implement small, manageable changes. Starting with just a 10-minute segment devoted to a priority task can generate momentum without overwhelming your system. These small wins compound over time, reinforcing the habit loop with positive feedback and increasing your confidence in managing Chronos rather than being controlled by it.

We live in an era awash with distractions that chip away at focus and fragment our temporal experience. Here, routines offer an anchor, but one that must be flexible enough to navigate shifting priorities. Imagine a routine as a river channel: strong and continuous, but capable of expanding or contracting to maintain flow even when rocks or debris temporarily block the way. This adaptiveness is what keeps routines sustainable long-term.

Moreover, it's essential to adopt a compassionate mindset about setbacks or deviations. No routine, however well-designed, can guarantee perfect adherence. Life flows unpredictably. Stress, illness, or unexpected opportunity may interfere. Instead of rigid moral judgments on lapses, view them as signals - indications that something in your routine needs recalibration. This approach turns "failure" into feedback, preserving motivation and curiosity rather than eroding it.

Professional lives often demand a certain uniformity of time management, but creatives and lifelong learners benefit enormously from recognizing the tension between structure and freedom. Routines don't have to be sterile templates that crush exploration. Instead, they can serve as scaffolding - providing enough order to help focus attention but enough breathing room to let imagination and growth emerge. The masterful balance lies in knowing when to stick to the routine and when to bend it or step away.

One practical method is to integrate periodic reviews of your routines. Setting aside time every week or month to reflect on what's working, what feels cumbersome, and where spontaneity can find more space builds a habit of mindful adjustment. This is not a one-time fix but a dynamic process of aligning your use of Chronos with evolving goals and life circumstances. Such reflective practice transforms routines from rigid timetables into living guides.

Discipline, then, need not be drudgery. When we harness Chronos with a flexible heart, the discipline serves our highest intentions rather than crushing them. It's the difference between a soldier's rigid march and a dancer's flowing movement - both rely on timing, but only one becomes a living art. Creating sustainable routines without stifling flexibility means holding this paradox: commitment and freedom, order and adaptation, structure and fluidity - all intertwined to empower a life lived fully and purposefully within time's embrace.

Chapter 10: Cultivating Kairos for Personal Growth

Unlocking Kairos - the opportune, rich moments that invite transformation - requires more than just awareness; it demands a cultivated sensitivity and readiness to embrace change when it arises. This means tuning into the subtle rhythms of life, trusting intuition, and allowing space for spontaneity within the structured flow of our daily routines. When you intentionally foster an openness to Kairos, you invite experiences that stretch beyond routine productivity into realms of deep personal insight and authentic growth. It's in these moments that fulfillment often sparks, as Kairos challenges us to pivot, rethink, and act in alignment with our highest potential. Cultivating this quality isn't a one-time skill but an evolving journey that redefines how we perceive time - not as a series of ticking seconds, but as a living, breathing landscape rich with possibility and meaning.

Practices to Increase Awareness and Readiness for Kairos

Recognizing and embracing Kairos moments requires more than just an intellectual understanding; it calls for a cultivated state of awareness. These are the moments when time feels full of potential - brief windows that quietly open and invite us to act with purpose, intuition, and clarity. To prepare ourselves for these moments, we need specific practices that sharpen our senses, deepen our presence, and tune us into the quieter rhythms of life. Increasing readiness for Kairos is ultimately about developing a deeper sensitivity to time beyond what the clock measures - a place where timing, choice, and chance come into alignment.

One foundational practice is mindfulness. Not just meditation or moments of silence, but a committed way of noticing. When we live by the rigid flow of Chronos, we tend to miss the subtleties that signal Kairos is near. Mindfulness reclaims attention from distraction and habit, allowing us to notice shifts in energy, intuition, or surroundings. For professionals and creatives alike, this kind of attention builds clarity and adaptability - two qualities that allow us to meet unexpected opportunities with focus and intention.

Reflective journaling is another valuable tool. Writing regularly creates a space where observation and intuition begin to meet. As we put thoughts and emotions into words, we start to notice patterns - threads of insight that might otherwise stay buried. Journaling becomes a way to translate the intuitive into something visible. Over time, it strengthens the inner voice and helps us listen more closely to signals we might otherwise dismiss. This isn't about planning every move - it's about staying inwardly prepared to meet the right moment when it comes.

Stillness, especially amid movement, is another powerful practice. In a culture driven by output and constant motion, pausing can feel unnatural - or even inefficient. But intentional stillness interrupts momentum just enough to let something new arise. It doesn't require hours. It can be a breath between tasks, a moment of quiet before a meeting, a phone set down during a walk. These pauses create openings - spaces where insight and readiness can take root.

Emotional awareness also plays a critical role. Kairos moments often carry a subtle emotional charge - a kind of quiet urgency or energy that signals something is shifting. Tuning into those feelings, and learning to trust them, makes a difference. You might feel an unexpected spark of excitement, or a physical sense of calm clarity. These sensations are guideposts. They don't always come with explanations, but they often arrive just in time to help us step into something meaningful.

Deep listening strengthens this sensitivity. This means listening to people, yes - but also to context, to the environment, to what isn't being said. Listening without agenda or expectation builds a kind of inner stillness that makes room for Kairos to emerge. When you listen in this way, conversations become more than exchanges - they become openings. What might have been a routine moment turns into a spark, a pivot, an invitation.

External habits can also support Kairos readiness. Flexible routines - as opposed to rigid schedules - leave room for insight, play, and unexpected turns. That might look like unstructured time in your calendar, or space for walking, reflection, or physical movement. These open pockets of time allow new ideas to rise to the surface. They keep you from being locked into a pattern that can't shift, even when something within you is ready for change.

Setting intention is another underrated practice. Kairos doesn't come just because we wait for it - it responds to readiness. Clarifying what you care about, where your energy wants to go, or what you're open to can help Kairos find you. Intentions don't have to be rigid. In fact, they work best when they're honest and flexible. They guide attention, steady motivation, and help the right moments feel familiar when they arrive.

Equally important is the ability to take risks - to step forward even when not everything is clear. Kairos rarely arrives with perfect conditions. Often, it asks you to trust timing before you can fully see where it's leading. That trust builds over time, especially when you learn to treat setbacks not as failures, but as part of the learning process. Missing a Kairos moment isn't the end - it's an invitation to stay alert and ready for the next.

When these practices are layered together - mindfulness, journaling, stillness, emotional awareness, deep listening, flexible routines, intention-setting, and courageous action - something changes. Your sense of time softens. The day no longer feels like a sequence of tasks, but something more fluid, more alive. You begin to notice what calls for your attention - not out of pressure, but from presence.

The shift isn't dramatic all at once. It builds quietly. You find yourself responding to opportunities more intuitively, making choices that feel both timely and grounded. You start to move with time instead of against it. Kairos becomes less elusive - not something rare or magical, but something woven into daily life, waiting for your readiness to meet it.

Preparing for Kairos isn't about chasing perfect moments. It's about learning to recognize what's already within reach. As you tune your awareness, build habits that support presence, and develop trust in your own timing, you create a life more responsive to change, more open to insight, and more aligned with what matters.

In that space, time shifts. It stops being something to manage or escape from. It becomes something you move with - a companion, not a constraint.

Life Stories Demonstrating Kairos-Driven Transformation

Throughout history and across different walks of life, people have found themselves standing at crossroads where the ordinary flow of chronological time, or Chronos, gives way to a Kairos moment - a critical point in time charged with opportunity, meaning, and possibility. It is in these moments that transformation can ignite, reshaping identities, goals, and trajectories. This section highlights several compelling life stories that bring Kairos into focus, showing how recognizing and embracing these unique pockets of time can lead to profound growth and fulfillment.

Consider Maya, a mid-career creative director stuck in a rigid corporate environment. Each day blended into the next, filled with back-to-back meetings and deadlines that slowly drained her sense of purpose. Then, during a seemingly ordinary company retreat, she took part in a spontaneous workshop on storytelling in advertising. It sparked something. This was a Kairos moment - a sudden convergence of inspiration, timing, and readiness. That experience lit a new path, and soon she began a side project centered on authentic, values-driven narratives. What began as a spark led to a major pivot, ultimately steering her toward a more meaningful and impactful creative path. Her openness to that moment shifted her course.

What gives Kairos its power isn't just the timing of events, but the inner readiness to see and act on them. Michael, a seasoned entrepreneur, had built a stable business over the course of a decade. Life was comfortable. Predictable. But a chance meeting at an industry event with a technologist exploring disruptive models challenged everything he thought he knew. Rather than brushing off the new ideas as risky or impractical, he chose to engage. He shifted gears, sacrificing some short-term gains to enter an unfamiliar, high-potential space. That decision reinvigorated not only his company, but his own sense of vision. The Kairos moment didn't change the external world overnight - it reawakened his commitment to innovation.

Not all Kairos moments arrive dramatically. Many appear as quiet shifts, easy to ignore. Sarah, a lawyer with a prestigious title and a calendar full of clients, had long defined success by hours billed and cases won. But then she volunteered on a legal aid project and found herself listening to a client in crisis. That conversation stirred something deeper - a sense that her skills could be used for more than just courtroom victories. That subtle inner stirring became a turning point. She eventually retrained as a mediator and redirected her legal career toward advocacy and justice. This wasn't a collapse of her old life, but a realignment toward something that had been calling to her for a long time.

Each of these stories shows that Kairos is not just about what happens around us - it's about how we respond. It is perception and presence that transform chance into choice. Growth, in these moments, comes from a decision to pause, to listen, and to shift direction even when the path is uncertain.

Marcus's story offers a more internal kind of Kairos. A software engineer known for efficiency and structure, Marcus was defined by deadlines and delivery cycles. But a health scare forced him to slow down. During recovery, one quiet afternoon changed everything - sunlight through a window, the silence of a room, a sudden shift in awareness. It wasn't dramatic, but it was real. He began to integrate mindfulness into his workday, not as a break from productivity but as a foundation for it. His outlook shifted. His software projects began to center on user empathy and well-being, illustrating how Kairos moments can transform how we work, not just why we work.

Kairos also shows up in how we move through failure. Janelle, a driven founder, saw her startup collapse after years of effort. The loss felt complete. But at a community event, she struck up a conversation with another entrepreneur who shared a story of resilience. That exchange was small - a few minutes, a few words - but it was enough. A door opened. Janelle began to see her experience not as defeat, but as groundwork. She channeled her learning into building a nonprofit that helps young founders navigate early failures. Her Kairos moment didn't erase the hardship. It transformed the meaning of it.

Some Kairos moments center on human connection. David, a high-performing executive, had grown distant from his teenage daughter. Their relationship had narrowed into brief, formal conversations. But after a family emergency, they shared a late-night talk that broke the pattern. In that unplanned space, David saw the weight of his absence and the depth of his daughter's need. That moment - raw and unstructured - reshaped how he approached parenting. He let go of striving for control and instead focused on trust, presence, and care. Their relationship changed, slowly but unmistakably. Kairos had opened a door, and he had walked through.

These stories remind us that Kairos moments don't always come with loud signals or dramatic shifts. Often, they appear as interruptions to our routines - a sudden sense of clarity, a quiet shift in feeling, a nudge to take a different route. The challenge is not only to notice, but to allow them in. When we're willing to pause, reflect, and act without full certainty, we create room for transformation.

There is a common thread through all of these examples - the interplay between the external and the internal. Kairos may present itself as an event, a conversation, or a disruption, but it becomes meaningful only when met with presence and readiness. That moment of choice - to follow the signal or ignore it - is where transformation takes root.

Elena's story captures this beautifully. A schoolteacher nearing burnout, she stumbled into a local writing group at the urging of a friend. One evening, she read aloud a short story from her journal. In that moment, she rediscovered her voice - not as a teacher, but as a human being with a story to tell. That shift carried into her classroom, where she started designing experiences that invited vulnerability and creativity. Her teaching changed, and so did her students. A small moment of expression became a source of renewed energy and deeper purpose.

These stories point to a larger truth: Kairos is not reserved for rare or extraordinary circumstances. It is woven through everyday life. The question is whether we are open to it. Transformation doesn't require waiting for perfect timing - it asks us to meet time with attention and courage.

As you reflect on your own life, ask yourself where Kairos might have already shown up. Were there moments that whispered rather than shouted? Did you sense an opening and walk past it, or did you pause long enough to step into something new?

Kairos is always close by. It doesn't replace Chronos, but it invites you to dance with time differently - to move beyond the boundaries of routine and into the possibility that something more meaningful might be waiting in the margins.

Chapter 11: The Dynamics of Time in Relationships

In every meaningful connection, time reveals itself as both a foundation and a fluid force, shaping how we relate and respond to one another. The structured rhythm of chronological time grounds us in shared routines and expectations, providing a framework where trust and reliability can grow. Yet, it is the elusive, opportune moments - the Kairos - that breathe vitality and depth into communication, allowing empathy and understanding to blossom unexpectedly.

Navigating between these dimensions requires emotional intelligence and presence, a willingness to honor schedules without losing sight of the spontaneous pulses that create genuine intimacy. When we learn to dance with time's dual nature, we unlock the power to transform relationships from mere transactions into synergistic partnerships that evolve in rhythm with life's unfolding realities. This dynamic interplay invites us to recognize timing as not just external but deeply internal, reflecting our readiness to connect authentically and expand our shared humanity.

Chronos gives structure to our commitments. It allows us to show up, to be dependable, to sync our calendars and plan our days. In relationships - professional, personal, or creative - this kind of timekeeping builds a baseline of mutual respect. Being on time, following through, and honoring agreements may seem ordinary, but these practices form the scaffolding that supports trust. When we consistently show up in Chronos, we create the conditions where connection can take root.

But what makes relationships grow is rarely the schedule itself. The turning points often happen in unscripted moments - the conversation that lingers beyond the meeting, the shared glance that communicates more than words, the unexpected vulnerability that deepens trust. These are Kairos moments - not planned, not forced, but full of potential because we are fully present. They emerge when we pause long enough to listen beyond the surface, to notice what is unfolding between the lines.

Emotional attunement plays a key role here. The ability to read tone, body language, or subtle shifts in energy can open the door to Kairos. It's not just about waiting for the right time, but about sensing it - an intuitive recognition that something meaningful is ready to happen. This requires us to let go of the script, to stop checking the clock, and to give space for what's real to emerge. Without this openness, we risk missing the small, powerful moments that build real connection.

In professional settings, the dominance of Chronos can create blind spots. Meetings are scheduled back to back, conversations are focused on deliverables, and interactions often prioritize efficiency over depth. While timelines and goals matter, so does the space in between. Leaders who understand the value of Kairos make room for unstructured dialogue, quiet reflection, and emotional resonance. They recognize that trust, creativity, and collaboration flourish not only under pressure, but in the moments where people feel seen and heard.

The same holds true in personal relationships. Calendars help us organize time together, but it is the Kairos moments - the unguarded laugh, the long pause, the unplanned detour - that infuse those hours with meaning. Relationships grow not just by spending time, but by sharing presence. And presence cannot be scheduled. It has to be offered, moment to moment, with openness and intention.

The balance between Chronos and Kairos in communication is especially visible in moments of conflict or transition. When tensions rise, it's easy to default to Chronos - to push for resolution, to stay on track, to get back to normal. But these moments often call for a different rhythm. Kairos invites us to slow down, to feel more deeply, to allow space for truths that don't fit neatly into bullet points. Healing and clarity often arrive not through speed or control, but through presence and timing that cannot be forced.

This awareness also supports boundary setting. Recognizing when to step back, when to pause a conversation, or when the timing simply isn't right helps preserve the integrity of the relationship. Just as Kairos can open a door, it can also signal when not to enter. Discernment matters - knowing that sometimes the most respectful thing we can do is wait, listen, and trust that the right moment will come.

Building relationships that honor both dimensions of time means practicing rhythm. It means showing up on time and being willing to linger. It means honoring agendas while staying open to what arises. It means letting Kairos moments interrupt the expected flow when something more important is ready to emerge. This rhythm doesn't follow a formula - it follows presence.

The more fluent we become in this rhythm, the more ease we find in human connection. We no longer rush past Kairos in the name of productivity, nor do we lose ourselves in waiting indefinitely for the perfect moment. Instead, we stay grounded in Chronos while attuned to Kairos - creating space for connection that is not only reliable, but alive.

In this way, time itself becomes a kind of conversation. Chronos says, "Show up." Kairos says, "Be here." And when both voices are heard, relationships become more than coordinated efforts. They become living exchanges shaped by respect, curiosity, and the courage to be present when it matters most.

Chronos and Kairos in Communication and Connection

When we consider relationships and communication, time often feels like an invisible thread weaving everything together. But not all time is created equal. At the heart of how we connect lies the dynamic interplay between two fundamental dimensions of time: Chronos and Kairos. Understanding the difference between these two can transform not only how we relate to others but also the depth and meaning of those interactions.

Chronos is what most people think of when they hear the word "time." It is sequential, quantitative, and measurable - the ticking clock, the calendar dates, the schedule you have to keep. This is the time that organizes much of our day-to-day communication in relationships, especially in professional or structured settings. Meetings start at 9 a.m., deadlines fall on Friday, lunch breaks last 60 minutes. It gives us a framework to coordinate with others efficiently.

Chronos governs the mechanics of connection. It helps us set expectations and boundaries. Without it, chaos would reign as we struggle to align our availability or know when it is appropriate to engage. Think about a phone call or video meeting scheduled ahead - the power of Chronos ensures both parties are on the same page about when to interact.

But Chronos alone does not capture the full essence of communication. This is where Kairos steps in, introducing a different dimension altogether. Kairos is qualitative, not quantitative. It is the opportune moment - the right time filled with meaning and charged with potential. It is not about clock hours or minutes; it is about timing that resonates deeply, emotionally, and contextually. In relationships, Kairos shows up as those spontaneous windows where connection feels natural, profound, and effortless.

Imagine a conversation where, despite no scheduled agenda or strict time limit, the discussion flows authentically. Both participants intuitively sense when to pause, when to listen, and when to speak up. These moments are Kairos in action. They defy the constraints of the clock but communicate more truth and feeling than any rigid timeframe could allow.

Recognizing and embracing Kairos in communication means tuning into the unspoken - the pauses, body language, and emotional undertones that tell us more than words alone. It involves being present and alert, understanding when a particular comment or gesture lands just right. This readiness to engage at the right moment, rather than strictly on schedule, is essential for building trust and intimacy.

In professional relationships, especially, the balance between Chronos and Kairos is critical to effective communication. Too much Chronos can lead to rigid conversations where parties focus strictly on time management, task completion, and hitting bullet points, often at the expense of genuine understanding. Meetings become mechanical; emails come across as impersonal; collaboration suffers because the right moment for creativity or honest feedback is never acknowledged.

Conversely, relying solely on Kairos without regard for Chronos can cause missed opportunities or confusion. Waiting for that perfect moment that never arrives can stall progress and frustrate everyone involved. The goal is not to favor one over the other but to harmonize these two temporal forces - to use Chronos as the structure and Kairos as the spirit of connection within it.

In intimate, personal relationships, Kairos takes on even greater importance. Life does not always fit neatly into schedules. The depth of emotional connection often grows in rare, meaningful instances when conditions align just right - when vulnerability feels safe to express, when empathy is ripe to be received, or when silence between partners speaks louder than words. These Kairos moments cannot be forced. They demand patience, openness, and trust that the right moment will come and be recognized.

This is why so many misunderstandings and conflicts arise when people try to impose Chronos-driven expectations on themselves and others without appreciating Kairos. For example, rushing to resolve a disagreement just because time is short can stifle genuine reconciliation. The opportunity for healing might have passed unnoticed, lost in the rush. Conversely, waiting indefinitely for the right time without communicating can breed resentment and stall growth.

But what if we could become more skilled in sensing Kairos? What if we learned to move beyond the mechanical ticking and tune ourselves to the rhythms of relationship time, finding the moments that spark true connection? Cultivating this sensitivity takes awareness and intention. It means stepping away from distractions and impatience, embracing stillness, and listening - not just with ears, but with heart and mind combined.

When we do, the rewards are real. Communication deepens. Empathy grows. Barriers fall away as people feel truly seen and heard. More importantly, relationships enter a new layer of meaning where time feels less like something to manage and more like something we are invited to experience.

This interplay of Chronos and Kairos also invites us to rethink how we approach conflict and resolution. Instead of viewing disagreements as problems to fix on a strict timeline, we can begin to understand timing as part of the equation. Sometimes, giving space and allowing Kairos to emerge leads to breakthroughs that no scheduled intervention ever could. It is about learning when to speak, when to listen, and when to wait. This awareness transforms conflict into opportunity.

Another layer of this communication balance lies in the nonverbal. Body language, eye contact, and presence operate in a space where Kairos thrives. The timing of a smile, the pause before responding, or the subtle mirroring of movement - these cues carry meaning that surpasses language. Here, Chronos may help us know when to begin the meeting, but Kairos fills the meeting with human connection.

In today's tightly structured world, the challenge is that technology and systems often lean hard on Chronos. Calendars, notifications, and to-do lists keep us on track, but they can also crowd out the slower, subtler rhythms of Kairos. True connection does not always appear in scheduled time slots. It emerges in the spaces we protect for presence, spontaneity, and attention.

Imagine a manager who keeps their team meetings efficient but stays just a few minutes afterward to check in more personally. Or a friend who sends a message not just because it is a birthday, but because they felt the moment was right. These are small acts that reflect Kairos awareness - moments of authentic timing that leave lasting impact.

Families, too, benefit from this balance. Tucking children into bed on schedule is a Chronos act. But choosing to pause and listen to their questions, even when it is late, is a Kairos choice. It teaches that some of the most meaningful moments do not follow a clock - they follow presence.

The paradox of Chronos and Kairos is that while they seem to pull in different directions, they actually work best together. Chronos gives us the structure to show up. Kairos helps us decide how to truly be there. The more we learn to honor both, the more powerful our communication becomes - not just efficient, but full of meaning.

In this way, we move beyond simply managing our time and begin inhabiting it. We show up for what matters. We listen for when it matters. And we respond in ways that let others know they matter. That is the heart of meaningful connection - and it begins by recognizing what kind of time each moment calls for.

Timing and Emotional Intelligence in Interactions

In the landscape of relationships, timing isn't just about when we speak or act; it's a subtle language that emotional intelligence helps us decode. The ability to sense when to engage, pause, or step back often determines the quality and depth of our connections. Timing, when fused with emotional intelligence, becomes a powerful tool, enabling us to navigate the complex rhythms of human interaction with grace and insight.

Emotional intelligence, at its core, is the aptitude to recognize, understand, and manage our own emotions while also empathizing with others'. It provides the compass needed to read social cues and adjust our timing accordingly. When we're emotionally attuned, we pick up on the invisible signals - the slight hesitation before someone speaks, the tension in a person's tone, or the joyful spark in an unexpected moment. These cues guide our timing, helping us to respond in a way that fosters trust rather than causing disruption.

Consider a professional meeting, where a thoughtful pause before responding can signal respect and reflection. Rushing to reply might seem like enthusiasm, but it can also come across as impatience or disregard. In contrast, emotional intelligence teaches us that perfect timing includes silence and listening, allowing space for others to express themselves fully. It's that balance between action and stillness that nurtures collaborative dialogue and meaningful exchanges.

The same principles apply in creative collaborations. Here, timing can mean waiting for the moment when inspiration flows naturally rather than forcing ideas prematurely. Emotional intelligence allows participants to sense the emotional temperature of the group, recognizing when tension is high or when excitement energizes everyone. This awareness creates an environment where creative Kairos moments - those ripe opportunities for breakthrough - can emerge, often in sync with intuitive timing rather than clock-driven schedules.

On a more personal level, intimate relationships demand a nuanced understanding of timing infused with emotional awareness. Reacting instantly to a loved one's upset might be instinctive, but pausing to assess emotional undertones can transform the response into something nurturing rather than reactive. Emotional intelligence encourages recognizing not only the words spoken but also the feelings behind them, which often arrive before any explicit expression. Tuning into this subtle timing helps avoid misunderstandings and fosters deeper connection.

Interestingly, timing in interactions involves more than just the moment of communication; it also encompasses the broader temporal context - the history shared, the present circumstances, and future expectations embedded within each encounter. Emotional intelligence enables us to factor these layers in, appreciating how past experiences might shape reactions and how future hopes influence present openness. This temporal sensitivity means recognizing when a conversation might unlock growth or when it risks reopening wounds.

There's also a rhythm to emotional expression within conversations. Emotional intelligence helps us to ride the flow rather than fight it - knowing when to push for honesty and when to offer gentleness. Imagine a situation where delivering critical feedback is necessary. The emotional timing becomes crucial; offering it when someone is overwhelmed might shut down communication, whereas choosing a moment when they're receptive leads to growth and improvement. It requires a finely tuned emotional radar to identify these windows of opportunity where timing maximizes positive impact.

Beyond individual interactions, groups and teams function on collective emotional timing. Leaders who cultivate emotional intelligence can sense the mood shifts within their teams, recognizing when to accelerate a project, when to pause and regroup, or when to celebrate small victories to boost morale. Timing here aligns with an understanding of collective emotional states, helping to sync group dynamics with external demands. The result is an environment where productivity and psychological safety coexist harmoniously.

In professional settings, being mindful of timing also mitigates conflict. Emotional intelligence aids in detecting early signs of frustration or disengagement, allowing timely interventions to prevent escalation. It's often about choosing not only what to say but when it's best to remain silent, giving emotions time to settle before revisiting difficult topics. This dynamic timing is a subtle form of emotional regulation practiced on interpersonal and organizational levels.

Learning this skill involves cultivating patience and self-awareness. Emotional intelligence teaches us that our internal urgency to respond or act doesn't always match the ideal timing outside ourselves. Developing a pause between feeling and reaction allows room for the best moment to emerge naturally. In essence, we learn that time in relationships isn't just measured by minutes or hours; it's the unfolding of emotional readiness and receptivity.

There's a paradox embedded in this practice: while Chronos - the clock time - keeps us moving forward, effective timing in interactions often requires stepping outside of this linear framework. Emotional intelligence invites us into Kairos - an opportune moment filled with qualitative meaning rather than quantitative measurement. Recognizing a Kairos moment means trusting intuition augmented by emotional awareness, a capacity that grows stronger with practice and reflection.

Mastering this interplay has profound implications for personal and professional growth. When we navigate timing with emotional intelligence, interactions transform from transactional exchanges into opportunities for trust-building, healing, and inspiration. We stop imposing rigid schedules on relationships and start honoring the natural rhythms that connect us at a deeper level. This awareness leads to greater harmony, enhancing not only the flow of communication but also the authenticity of connection.

It's worth noting that emotional intelligence's role in timing isn't about perfection or manipulation but about responsiveness and respect. Misjudgments will happen, and moments will be missed, but each experience offers insight into refining this delicate balance. The journey involves tuning into what's happening beneath the surface while aligning action with the flow of shared time. It's this dance of awareness and timing that enriches relationships over time.

At the heart of these dynamics lies a spiritual dimension to time's passage within human connection. Moments charged with emotional resonance often transcend ordinary chronology, allowing us to feel the presence of something larger - a shared understanding, an alignment of values, or a silent bond. Emotional intelligence helps us access these moments by opening our sensitivity to the unseen currents that shape timing.

So, developing emotional intelligence isn't merely a soft skill but a form of time mastery. It enables us to synchronize our internal clocks with those of others, fostering interactions that honor both Chronos and Kairos. This integration invites us to become more intentional with our presence, choosing not only what to say but when to say it, amplifying the significance of every encounter.

By embracing timing alongside emotional awareness, we dissolve many barriers to effective communication. Relationships begin to thrive, whether in the office, studio, or home, because the flow of interaction respects the subtle pulses of human emotion. This wisdom invites a profound shift - from managing time as an external resource to living it as a shared experience shaped by empathy and insight.

Ultimately, timing and emotional intelligence in interactions guide us toward a more fulfilling use of time itself. They remind us that the moments we share with others are not just points on a schedule but living opportunities to connect, grow, and evolve together. Navigating this terrain wisely can illuminate the pathways to richer, more meaningful relationships in every area of life.

Chapter 12: Technology, Time, & the Modern Dilemma

In an age where technology promises to save us time, it often ends up fragmenting it - pulling our attention in countless directions and blurring the lines between Chronos and Kairos. Digital tools shape our experience of time by accelerating the pace of life, yet they can also mask the true value of meaningful moments, making it harder to recognize Kairos when it appears. The modern dilemma is clear: while technology grants unprecedented access and efficiency, it also demands discipline and awareness to prevent the erosion of presence and deep focus.

Embracing technology consciously means learning to channel its power without becoming enslaved by constant connectivity - ultimately reclaiming the spaciousness needed for Kairos to emerge even amid the digital clutter. This balance unlocks not only productivity but a richer, fuller engagement with life's fleeting opportunities.

How Digital Tools Influence Our Experience of Chronos and Kairos

In our fast-paced modern world, digital tools have reshaped how we interact with time itself, particularly the ancient yet ever-relevant concepts of Chronos and Kairos. Chronos is the measurable, sequential time that ticks relentlessly forward. Kairos, by contrast, refers to the opportune moment when everything aligns for meaningful action. Both take on new dimensions through the screens and devices that dominate our days. These tools offer remarkable benefits in organizing the linear flow of Chronos, yet they also challenge our ability to recognize and embrace Kairos moments. The tension between these two experiences has become one of the defining dilemmas of technology's role in our lives.

To begin with, digital calendars, reminders, and project management apps excel at framing our lives within Chronos. They slice our hours into blocks, define deadlines, and help ensure accountability within a rigid schedule. This fosters greater productivity and allows us to plan personal and professional goals with clarity. But this same structuring often pushes Kairos - the spontaneous, transformative moment - to the margins. When every minute is pre-assigned, it leaves little room for the uncharted territory where Kairos resides. The convenience of digital time management can paradoxically narrow the space needed for the unpredictable opportunities that don't appear on a calendar.

At the same time, these platforms can dull our sensitivity to Kairos moments. Notifications ping constantly, flooding our attention with distractions that fragment concentration. The urgency of alerts driven by Chronos often drowns out the quieter signals that let us know a Kairos moment may be near. When our devices train us to react rather than reflect, it becomes harder to stay present and receptive. We lose touch with the kind of experiential time that Kairos evokes.

Even so, technology holds potential to support Kairos - if used intentionally. Digital tools can be harnessed to create space instead of simply filling it. Mindfulness apps, digital detox settings, and timers designed to encourage deep work followed by reflection can help recalibrate our relationship with time. These tools serve as gentle nudges to slow down, focus, and notice moments that carry significance beyond efficiency. In doing so, they foster environments where Kairos can emerge rather than be overlooked.

Technology also expands the possibility of Kairos through rapid connectivity. The ability to collaborate instantly and share ideas in real time opens new windows for insight and innovation. These opportunities don't rely on physical presence - they travel across networks, surfacing when timing, receptivity, and context align. This makes Kairos more accessible in certain ways, but also more vulnerable to misinterpretation. Just because something is fast or widespread doesn't mean it holds depth. The quality of engagement still matters. True Kairos demands readiness, not just reach.

Our growing dependence on digital timekeeping also influences how we relate to memory and anticipation. As devices store schedules, reminders, and histories, we outsource much of our internal sense of time. While this reduces mental strain, it can dull the inner awareness that once helped us feel the right moment to act. The more we rely on alerts to tell us what to do, the easier it is to forget how to sense Kairos from within. This shift calls for reflection: how do we balance technological convenience with the preservation of intuitive timing?

There is also the role of digital storytelling and social media in shaping shared Kairos experiences. Moments that were once private or fleeting now unfold publicly, often generating collective attention in real time. Viral movements, virtual gatherings, and live streams can create a sense of communal timing. When many people focus on a single moment, it can carry weight and resonance. Still, this collective Kairos only holds meaning if approached with authenticity. When attention becomes performative, we risk diluting the very moment we hope to elevate.

For professionals and creatives, the opportunity lies in learning to use digital tools as allies rather than distractions. Protecting open space in a digital calendar allows for spontaneity. Turning off nonessential notifications helps restore mental stillness. Journaling apps, voice memos, or digital prompts can bring awareness to Kairos moments that might otherwise go unrecognized. These habits invite us to use technology as a support structure that respects both linear order and creative emergence.

At the same time, we must stay aware of tech-driven overload. The constant pressure to be responsive, visible, and productive can reduce time to a metric - something to optimize, monetize, and track. This mindset leaves little space for mystery or meaning. The antidote lies in cultivating a more mindful relationship with time. When we treat digital tools as extensions of intention rather than authorities, we gain the freedom to choose when to align with Chronos and when to make space for Kairos.

It's also important to remember that Kairos cannot be forced. No app or algorithm can summon the perfect moment to speak, act, or create. These moments must unfold naturally. While technology can facilitate Kairos, it often works best when used sparingly - as a framework that supports, not a force that dictates. The goal is to bridge the quantitative order of Chronos with the qualitative sensitivity of Kairos in a way that honors both.

In the end, technology's impact on our experience of time is not inherently good or bad. It enhances our ability to navigate Chronos with speed and clarity, but it also challenges our capacity to inhabit Kairos with presence and depth. The key lies in conscious use - building digital practices that support productivity without eclipsing spontaneity. When we succeed in this, digital tools become not just timekeepers, but time-shapers, helping us access both efficiency and meaning.

This kind of balance is what allows time to work for us rather than against us. It opens the door to a fuller engagement with life - one where structure supports creativity and where every alert or pause holds the possibility of significance. By choosing to interact with technology mindfully, we reconnect with Kairos even in a world wired for Chronos, and in doing so, we rediscover time as something far richer than a series of tasks to be completed.

Strategies to Reclaim Kairos Amidst Technological Distraction

In today's digital age, where screens constantly compete for our attention, seizing Kairos moments has become increasingly challenging. The relentless ping of notifications, the endless scroll of social feeds, and the illusion of perpetual connectivity fragment our focus and steal the very instants ripe for meaningful engagement. But Kairos is not just about finding time. It's about recognizing and embracing opportunity, presence, and depth. It's time that breathes life into experience rather than just counting the minutes. Fortunately, reclaiming Kairos amid this technological haze isn't impossible. It requires deliberate strategies, a mindfulness of how technology impacts our rhythms, and a commitment to interrupt the habitual patterns that keep us tethered to superficial time.

One crucial step lies in curating the digital environment to support intentionality rather than distraction. The subconscious pull of endless apps and alerts thrives on default settings designed to capture attention at any cost. Turning off nonessential notifications can immediately reclaim mental space. When the inbox doesn't demand instant replies, and social media platforms stop flashing urgency with each new like or comment, a quieter mental horizon opens. This disconnection, paradoxically, restores connection to the present moment. Structuring focused time blocks during which technology is consciously limited - sometimes even fully disengaged - allows Kairos moments room to unfold naturally. These pockets of tech-free time serve as fertile ground where creativity, insight, and meaningful interaction can emerge unpressured by constant interruptions.

Beyond technological pruning, cultivating a state of receptivity becomes essential. Kairos moments often arise through subtle shifts in awareness rather than grand gestures or intentional goals. Developing openness means training the mind to slow down and become curious about what's happening right now, instead of racing ahead mentally or succumbing to distraction. Meditation, mindfulness practices, or simply pausing throughout the day can nurture this quality of presence. Even a brief glance away from the screen can lead to noticing opportunities that were previously invisible amid the noise. The skill lies in consistently observing where your attention lands and gently bringing it back when it wanders.

Interestingly, the tools of technology themselves can become partners in reclaiming Kairos - if used with care. Apps that support deep work, or reminders that prompt moments of mindfulness, can help guide attention back toward focus and reflection. The key is using them with awareness, avoiding the trap of replacing one form of distraction with another. The most effective approach is one where technology serves human rhythms rather than overriding them. Setting clear intentions before using digital tools - knowing what purpose your screen time will serve - turns passive consumption into conscious choice. This shift transforms technology from a source of fragmentation into a means of expanding kairotic potential.

Reimagining how we think about multitasking and busyness is another essential practice. The cultural obsession with doing multiple things at once directly undermines Kairos, which thrives on depth and presence. Schedules packed with overlapping tasks scatter attention and diminish the potential for flow or insight. Learning to embrace single-tasking - even in short intervals - fosters a state where Kairos can emerge. This might look like putting devices away during conversations, creative work, or meals, and offering full presence to the experience at hand. It not only elevates the quality of that experience but also honors Kairos as a vital dimension of time.

Intentional rest and solitude also play a crucial role. In a world saturated with digital noise, quiet and stillness can feel unfamiliar or even uncomfortable. Yet these pauses often become the spaces where Kairos moments form. Allowing time to simply be - without immediately filling every gap with entertainment or information - helps the mind reset. These still intervals let the subconscious connect ideas and process emotions beyond the linear logic of Chronos. Carving out regular screen-free downtime restores internal spaciousness and invites Kairos to rise to the surface.

Technology encourages immediacy. It promotes short-term reactions over long-term awareness. Reclaiming Kairos in this climate requires shifting from urgency to discernment. It means learning to pause before replying - creating space between stimulus and response. For professionals and creatives, this might look like resisting the impulse to answer every message instantly or checking email continuously throughout the day. Batching communications into set windows preserves larger segments of uninterrupted time for deeper work and reflection.

The social layer matters here as well. Many of our digital habits substitute fragmented interaction for genuine connection. Yet Kairos flourishes in presence - in the unscripted moments when timing, attention, and emotion align. Choosing to set aside devices when with others - putting phones away at meals or stepping into a conversation without distraction - signals value and respect. These small decisions make room for connection to unfold more fully. When we are present, opportunities for insight, shared meaning, and spontaneous joy often follow.

It's also important to embrace imperfection in this process. Slowing down may feel countercultural. Focus may falter. Some days, distractions win. But Kairos doesn't require perfection. It thrives in flexible rhythms, not rigid control. Developing a balanced relationship with time means holding both Chronos and Kairos with care. When we view distraction as a signal rather than a failure, we can gently shift back toward more meaningful engagement without shame or frustration.

Ultimately, Kairos blooms most fully when it aligns with what matters. That alignment becomes the foundation for reclaiming depth in a digitally scattered world. Reflecting regularly on your values, priorities, and intentions helps clarify which moments deserve your presence. Whether in work that excites your curiosity, relationships that nourish your spirit, or practices that cultivate peace, centering your time around what truly matters naturally makes space for Kairos. Technology, in this case, becomes a support rather than a barrier.

Reclaiming Kairos in the digital age is not about rejecting technology. It's about approaching it with mindfulness and clarity. By creating boundaries, deepening presence, and honoring the pauses in between, we invite Kairos to return - not as an escape from modern life, but as an essential part of it. This shift allows time to feel whole again. Focus becomes sharper. Relationships deepen. Creative energy flows with less resistance. In this balance, technology no longer fragments our days but becomes a tool to support a fuller, more intentional experience of time.

Chapter 13: Integrating Chronos & Kairos

Bringing Chronos and Kairos into harmony isn't about choosing one over the other, but about weaving them together to craft a life that's both productive and deeply meaningful. Chronos keeps us grounded with structure and order, helping us manage daily demands, while Kairos invites us to pause and embrace those fleeting, transformative moments that lead to breakthrough insights and authentic growth. When we learn to listen to the rhythms of both - the steady cadence of Chronos and the intuitive pull of Kairos - we unlock a powerful synergy. This allows us to align our schedules with our soul's calling, transforming routine into opportunity and chaos into clarity, ultimately empowering us to live each day fully engaged in purposeful action and timeless presence.

Creating a Personal Framework for Time Mastery

Time mastery isn't about controlling every second on the clock or cramming more tasks into your schedule. It's about developing a harmonious understanding of two distinct dimensions of time: Chronos - the quantitative, measurable component - and Kairos - the qualitative, opportune moments that bring meaning and potential to our lives. Creating a personal framework for time mastery means intentionally balancing these forces to move with purpose rather than just passively moving through time.

At its core, this framework starts with cultivating awareness - knowing not just when things happen, but why they happen at certain moments and how your engagement with time shapes your experience. This requires moving beyond seeing time as a relentless taskmaster and instead embracing it as a dynamic field where you can act with discernment and insight. Many professionals and creatives fall into the trap of living exclusively in Chronos, chasing deadlines and productivity metrics but missing the Kairotic bursts that fuel inspiration and meaning.

Building a personal time mastery framework involves establishing a set of guiding principles that honor both Chronos and Kairos. One of the first steps is reflection - taking stock of how you currently experience time. Do you feel ruled by a rigid schedule or overwhelmed by a calendar packed with back-to-back meetings? Or are you often caught in waiting, unsure when the right moment to act will come? This honest assessment shapes the foundation for change.

Once you understand your natural tendencies, you can craft strategies that weave Chronos and Kairos together rather than allowing them to compete. For example, while setting clear timelines and benchmarks for segments of your work or life is crucial, you must also remain open and attuned to those subtle Kairos windows - the unexpected flashes of insight or opportunity that defy clock-time but deeply influence quality and fulfillment. This dual approach shifts your relationship with time from reactive to proactive, empowering you to create space for flow and spontaneity within a structure that keeps you grounded.

It's also vital to recognize that this isn't a one-size-fits-all mold waiting to be filled. Everyone's relationship with Chronos and Kairos varies depending on personality, profession, and life circumstances. That's why crafting this framework demands customization. You must experiment with different rhythms to discover what mix of schedule and spontaneity fuels your best work and most fulfilling moments. Some may find anchoring their mornings in Chronos practices - strict start times, prioritized to-dos - while reserving afternoons for Kairos explorations most effective. Others might invert this balance.

Incorporating rituals is a powerful tool within this framework. Rituals serve as mindful time markers that honor both types of time. A morning ritual, for instance, can be a deliberate entry point into Chronos, setting intentions and organizing tasks. Meanwhile, midday pauses or creative breaks can be rituals in service of Kairos, offering time to listen inwardly and catch those precious moments of opportunity. Over time, these rituals create a rhythm that feels less like a race and more like a dance with time.

Another essential component is learning to interpret your intuition as a time compass. Kairos moments often arrive with a subtle nudge - a feeling, a prompt that something significant is unfolding now. Many dismiss these sensations in the rush of daily demands, yet they are perhaps the finest signals in mastering time. Honing your ability to sense and follow these internal cues allows you to step into Kairotic moments with readiness, amplifying your creative capacity and decision-making.

Embracing patience is equally critical to this framework. Kairos doesn't submit to schedules or pressure; it unfolds in its own timing. So cultivating the discipline to wait, to remain open and attentive without forcing outcomes, can feel like a counterintuitive effort compared to typical notions of productivity. Yet, it's in this space of patience that true mastery over time begins - knowing when to act and, importantly, when to hold back.

To deepen this mastery, integrating technology with discernment is necessary but tricky. Digital tools excel at managing Chronos - calendars, timers, reminders - but they easily drown Kairos in a flood of distractions. Designing intentional tech habits that protect your Kairotic space - such as scheduled digital detoxes or prioritized deep-focus sessions - helps maintain balance. Your framework should include clear boundaries that prevent Chronos-driven busyness from overwhelming the intuitive flow of Kairos.

Accountability, often overlooked, gives structure to time mastery without suffocating it. Whether driven by peer groups, coaches, or personal commitments, having regular checkpoints helps align your Chronos activities with your larger life vision and Kairos opportunities. These moments of review not only help in course correction but also cultivate gratitude for moments seized and lessons learned from those missed. Accountability becomes a catalyst for growth rather than a source of pressure.

Importantly, this framework needs to align deeply with your core values and long-term goals. Time mastery isn't an end in itself - it's a means to live purposefully. By consistently asking how your use of time reflects what truly matters to you, your framework evolves beyond efficiency and taps into meaning. This alignment transforms the way you perceive deadlines - not as constraints, but as guideposts leading toward your definition of a fulfilling life.

Consider the story of Sarah, a creative director who struggled for years under the tyranny of external deadlines and the relentless Chronos clock. By crafting and committing to a personal time mastery framework, she introduced morning rituals that carved out undisturbed planning time, embraced intuitive breaks to explore fresh ideas, and set tech boundaries to reduce interruptions. She paired this with weekly accountability sessions where she reflected on how her time investment served her overarching vision of cultivating innovation and balance in her team. Within months, Sarah noticed a shift - not only in her productivity but in her sense of purpose and satisfaction. She no longer felt enslaved by the clock but liberated by a framework that honored both measured time and moments rich with possibility.

Such transformations demonstrate that time mastery is a lifelong practice - a commitment to ongoing adjustment rather than a final destination. Your framework should be flexible enough to adapt as your life unfolds, yet stable enough to provide a reliable compass amid uncertainty. Each iteration strengthens your ability to navigate time's paradoxical nature, weaving Chronos and Kairos into a seamless fabric of living with intention and depth.

Ultimately, creating your personal framework for time mastery invites a profound shift in how you experience existence. It's an invitation to move from being hurried and fragmented toward becoming centered and whole, to live days that feel expansive and full rather than merely filled. When you learn to integrate the rhythm of clocks with the rhythm of opportunity, you unlock a way to meet time not as an adversary but as a wise ally - guiding you toward a more purposeful life.

Aligning Time Awareness with Life Goals and Values

When we talk about time, it's easy to get caught up in schedules, clocks, and deadlines - the domain of Chronos. But integrating an awareness of time that resonates deeply with your life's purpose means going beyond the ticking seconds. It's about aligning both Chronos and Kairos - the quantitative and the qualitative, the measured and the meaningful - with your most authentic goals and core values. This alignment transforms the way you experience time, turning it from a relentless taskmaster into a supportive guide that propels you toward a life well lived.

At the heart of this process lies a fundamental awareness: Time isn't just something to be managed, it's something to be honored. Most of us have a list of commitments pulling us in countless directions. But when you consistently reframe your relationship with time through the lens of your deeper aspirations, those tasks acquire new meaning. Instead of feeling like boxes to check off, they become stepping stones that move you closer to what truly matters. The difference is profound. Suddenly, time is no longer the enemy but an ally that respects your values.

To initiate this alignment, first consider your life goals - not as abstract ambitions but as living, breathing intentions that shape your daily choices. These goals need to be genuinely yours, not borrowed from societal expectations or fleeting trends. When your goals are rooted in authentic values, they form a compass that guides your time awareness toward significance rather than sheer productivity. This doesn't mean abandoning Chronos or neglecting schedules. Rather, it's about implementing a flexible framework where measured time supports meaningful time.

We live in a world obsessed with doing more, faster. The pressure to maximize minutes can blind us to Kairos moments - the rare, often unplanned opportunities that call for our intuition, presence, and readiness. Aligning time awareness with life goals means cultivating the ability to sense these Kairos windows and act deliberately when they appear. It's not a matter of controlling time but tuning in to its rhythms so that your responses harmonize with what feels right, timely, and aligned.

This harmony demands honesty. It invites you to ask blunt questions: Are the hours I'm investing each day moving me toward what I deeply value, or am I just reacting to external demands? How much of my time is dedicated to activities that nourish my purpose as opposed to feeding anxieties or distractions? By confronting these questions, you start disentangling Chronos-driven busyness from Kairos-infused engagement. There's a subtle but vital difference between being busy and being purposeful.

It helps to visualize your time as a living ecosystem where each element - tasks, relationships, reflection, rest - needs balance and nurturance. When time awareness syncs with your values, this ecosystem thrives. Your days gain texture beyond checklist completion, weaving moments that foster growth, connection, and meaning. This perspective gently counters the modern tendency to fragment time into isolated units. Instead, time becomes a flowing continuum shaped by what feels right in your heart and mind.

Consider the power of saying "no" as a form of alignment. This simple act is often underrated but profoundly impactful. It carves out the necessary space to honor your most essential priorities. Saying "no" isn't about rejection but about protection - guarding your time so that it serves your vision rather than dilutes it. Each deliberate no fortifies your capacity to recognize and embrace the Kairos moments that propel you toward fulfillment.

Another practical dimension of this alignment is how you set goals themselves. When goals reflect surface desires disconnected from true values, they can become traps that sustain a chronicle of stress and disillusionment. In contrast, values-centered goals - those that speak to your deeper self - infuse your relationship with time with energy and resilience. They encourage patience when progress is slow and celebrate breakthroughs that feel like invitations, not obligations.

Time awareness tied to your life's compass encourages you to rethink interruptions and quiet moments. Instead of viewing breaks or pauses as lost time, you start seeing them as fertile spaces, moments filled with potential. These intervals allow subconscious thoughts to rise, creativity to spark, and emotional recalibration to occur. Kairos thrives in these pauses, inviting you to seize opportunities that rigid planning misses.

The alignment process also extends to how you measure success in your use of time. Success determined solely by output or external approval can leave you feeling hollow. However, reframing success to include internal satisfaction and value consistency cultivates a sustainable drive that honors both Chronos and Kairos. You learn to celebrate progress and presence, equally recognizing the discipline of regular effort and the magic of inspired spontaneity.

This integration influences not only your personal path but your relationships. When your awareness of time fits with your values, your interactions gain depth and authenticity. You find yourself more present, responsive, and aware of timing's emotional nuances - whether it's offering support, having a tough conversation, or simply sharing silence. Time aligned with values creates stronger, more meaningful connections because it respects the rhythm of each person involved.

It's worth emphasizing that this alignment isn't a one-time achievement but an ongoing dialogue. Life evolves, and so do our priorities and perceptions of time. Periodic reflection becomes essential. Regularly tuning into your goals and values and recalibrating your relationship with time ensures that you stay on course. This rhythm of reflection and adjustment creates a dynamic balance rather than a rigid regime, supporting both discipline and flexibility - a coexistence of Chronos and Kairos in harmony.

Sometimes life will throw unexpected challenges that disrupt even the best-laid plans. Here, time awareness grounded in your values offers a stabilizing anchor. When external pressures mount, remembering your purpose helps navigate setbacks with grace rather than frustration. The measured patience of Chronos combined with the intuitive timing of Kairos cultivates resilience. You learn to hold your vision steady while adapting your steps, creating a purposeful dance with time's flow.

On a practical level, cultivating habits that reinforce this alignment can be transformative. Setting aside moments for intentional reflection, journaling about your evolving goals, or simply pausing before committing to new tasks allows you to check in with your internal compass. These simple practices create space to balance the demands of the clock with the quiet invitations of your inner self. Over time, this reorients your entire experience of time from reaction to creation.

The result is a life where time feels more expansive, rich with possibility rather than constricted by scarcity. You build the capacity to embrace both structure and spontaneity, recognizing each as gifts when directed by sincere purpose. The ability to integrate these dimensions of time nourishes creativity, deepens satisfaction, and enhances clarity in decision-making.

Ultimately, aligning time awareness with life goals and values demands courage and commitment. It asks you to step away from the illusion that time is merely a resource to be consumed and instead see it as an unfolding canvas shaped by intention, presence, and meaning. This shift invites a fuller involvement in your own story, where every moment offers the invitation to live in greater alignment with what matters most.

Chapter 14: Timelessness and the Illusion of Age

In a world that measures worth by youth and productivity, time becomes a silent adversary. Chronos, with its ticking precision, reduces aging to arithmetic, a countdown of years, milestones, and decline. Yet beneath this mechanistic rhythm flows Kairos, the soul's time, where aging is not loss but evolution, not a fading of potential but a deepening of wisdom.

Modern society teaches us to resist the natural unfolding of time, to fear its imprint on the body and equate its passage with diminishing relevance. The result is a collective hypnosis: we learn to dread the clock instead of listening to what it's trying to teach us. But the paradox of aging is not about biology alone - it's about belief. The stories we tell about time become the scripts our cells obey.

To master the illusion of age, we must first step out of Chronos and into Kairos, the dimension where meaning transcends measurement. Here, vitality is not reclaimed by fighting time, but by befriending it, by recognizing that every stage of life carries its own brilliance, resonance, and renewal. When we stop counting the years and start inhabiting the moments, we discover that timelessness is not a fantasy, but our natural state of being.

Overcoming the Expectations of Growing Old

Aging, in its truest sense, is not merely the passage of time but the interpretation of it. We are not defined by the years that pass but by the meaning we assign to them. The body, yes, shifts with experience. The skin records sunlight and laughter; the muscles remember effort and surrender. Yet beneath these visible changes lives something untouched and unchanging - a field of consciousness that remains ageless.

The way we perceive time determines how we experience aging. When we live through Chronos, we see life as a countdown: hours, years, achievements, deadlines. It is the clock-driven world that insists we measure, compare, and prove our worth through productivity. But when we shift into Kairos, time becomes an unfolding moment of meaning, presence, and resonance. Life is no longer something we race through; it becomes something we expand into.

Our culture worships youth as the pinnacle of vitality and fears the passing of years as a slow fading. This conditioning is so ingrained that many people experience aging as loss long before their bodies ever decline. We begin to anticipate decay instead of awakening. We start to defend against time instead of deepening into it. But what if the opposite were true? What if every year, every season, every so-called wrinkle of experience was an upgrade - a refinement of wisdom, alignment, and soul expression?

To live in Kairos is to reclaim this possibility. It is to awaken from the trance of aging as decline and remember that life's rhythm is one of continual renewal.

The Myth of Decline

The idea that aging equals deterioration is not an inherent biological truth; it is a belief — and a powerful one. From a Chronos perspective, time is a straight line leading from birth to death, and everything between is a gradual descent from vitality to frailty. We learn this script early. It becomes the background hum of our society: "When you're young, you can," "Once you hit forty, you can't," "After fifty, it's too late."

This narrative is not neutral; it's hypnotic. It imprints itself on our subconscious, creating self-fulfilling prophecies that affect how our cells behave, how our hormones regulate, how our minds adapt, and how our spirit expresses itself through the body.

Modern science is beginning to prove what the mystics and metaphysicians have always known: the mind is the architect of the body. Through the study of epigenetics, we now understand that our genes are not fixed scripts but dynamic expressions influenced by belief, emotion, and environment. Neuroplasticity shows that the brain continues to rewire and regenerate at every stage of life. And quantum biology reveals that the human body operates not only through chemical processes but through vibrational coherence — frequencies that respond directly to thought, emotion, and intention.

What this reveals is extraordinary: the way you speak about aging becomes the very message your body follows in how to express it.

If you tell your body, "We are running out of time," your cells rush to exhaustion.

If you tell your body, "There is no hurry; I am in the perfect moment," your biology harmonizes around renewal.

To age in Chronos is to measure your decline.
To age in Kairos is to amplify your awareness.

The Physiology of Timelessness

When we shift into Kairos, the entire physiology of the body begins to change.
This is not poetic exaggeration. It is measurable, observable, and profoundly transformative.

Chronos living keeps the nervous system in a state of vigilance. The constant mental chatter of "not enough time," "too late," or "I'm getting old" triggers stress hormones that accelerate cellular aging. Chronic urgency creates inflammation, shortens telomeres, and disrupts the delicate rhythms of the endocrine system. The body begins to believe it must survive rather than thrive.

Kairos, by contrast, activates the parasympathetic nervous system, the state of repair, regeneration, and restoration. When you are deeply present - when you meditate, create, connect, or simply breathe with awareness - the body interprets safety. The heart's electromagnetic field synchronizes, the brain waves slow and balance, and coherence spreads through every system. The result is not just calmness but vitality.

Studies in quantum coherence and consciousness-based medicine support what spiritual teachers have said for centuries: presence is regenerative. Moments of absorption, gratitude, awe, and love literally change the body's chemistry. They soften the pull of entropy, amplify vitality, and alter the very way time unfolds. In Kairos, the clock does not stop.

But your **experience** of it transforms.

Reframing the Seasons of Life

Chronos divides life into chapters - childhood, adulthood, midlife, old age - as though they were separate realms, each closing as another begins. But Kairos sees the seasons of life as cyclical, overlapping, and eternally evolving. Each phase carries its own sacred intelligence.

Youth is not the only season of growth; it is simply the first. Maturity brings refinement and mastery. Age brings integration, wisdom, and expanded awareness. Each stage contributes to the wholeness of being. When we stop fearing the transitions, we begin to recognize that every "ending" in Chronos is simply a rebirth in Kairos.

When we live in alignment with this rhythm, aging ceases to be a slow erosion of identity and becomes an awakening of essence. The years don't take away from you; they reveal you. Like rings in a tree, they are proof of strength, adaptation, and memory. The soul's timing is circular, not linear.

It returns again and again to what is essential until it is mastered, integrated, and expressed. And in that remembrance, there is no decline, only deepening.

Breaking the Spell of "Too Late"

The greatest illusion created by Chronos is the belief in "too late." It is one of the most destructive phrases in human language. It keeps people from changing careers, starting new loves, learning new skills, or following callings that have whispered for decades. It traps the spirit in regret and the body in contraction.

Yet the universe does not operate on deadlines. Energy moves according to readiness, not the clock. A soul awakening at sixty is no less divine than one at twenty. In Kairos, every moment is perfectly timed because it is aligned with awareness. When readiness meets opportunity, age dissolves. When courage meets intention, time expands.

Think of the countless creators who discovered their true power later in life - artists, healers, inventors, visionaries. What changed was not their body, but their belief. They began to trust the pulse of Kairos rather than the ticking of Chronos. They stopped chasing time and began to collaborate with it.

Kairos teaches that no dream, no healing, no purpose ever expires. It waits for the moment of alignment. And when that moment comes, it feels both spontaneous and inevitable, as though it was always waiting for you to remember it.

The Energetics of Youthfulness

To understand aging through Kairos is to realize that youthfulness is not an era of life but a frequency of being. You can be biologically sixty and vibrationally thirty. You can be twenty but energetically weary from decades of mental Chronos conditioning. Youthfulness is not stored in your cells; it is expressed through your consciousness.

Every time you laugh freely, forgive easily, or create without fear of failure, you access this frequency. Every act of presence sends a signal through the nervous system that says, "We are alive now." The body responds with vitality. The energy field brightens. The eyes regain their spark.

This is not denial of change. It is mastery of perception. When you live by Kairos, you move in rhythm with regeneration. You become a living reminder that time does not take from you - it reveals you.

Practices for Timeless Living

The mastery of time is not achieved through resistance but through rhythm. These practices help recondition your awareness from Chronos urgency to Kairos presence.

1. Pause the Clock

Several times a day, consciously disengage from the mental countdown. Close your eyes, breathe deeply, and ask, "Where am I in this moment?" Let yourself arrive fully in the now without needing to measure or manage it. This simple pause recalibrates your entire system.

2. Repattern the Narrative

Notice your internal dialogue about age and time. Replace thoughts such as "I'm getting old" with "I'm evolving." Language carries energy. Each word you speak becomes instruction to your body and field.

3. Practice Novelty and Curiosity

The mind stays young through curiosity. Learn something new, a movement, a language, a song. Novelty signals renewal to your neural networks and reawakens joy.

4. Embody Rhythm

Engage in activities that have rhythm rather than pace: dance, walk, swim, breathe, or garden. Rhythm aligns you with the flow of Kairos, reminding your body that time is cyclical, not competitive.

5. Connect with Nature

Spend time each day in natural light. Observe sunrise or sunset. The cycles of the earth recalibrate your circadian rhythms and remind your biology that all life renews in patterns, not in decline.

6. Dialogue with Your Timeless Self

In meditation or journaling, connect with the aspect of yourself that is beyond age. Ask this self for guidance. Listen for the wisdom that comes not from your years, but from your essence.

Kairos as the Fountain of Renewal

The mythic search for the fountain of youth has always been a metaphor for what Kairos truly represents: a state of timeless presence. It is not found in a place or product, but in awareness. You touch the fountain whenever you are so immersed in the moment that time dissolves. When you lose yourself in creativity, love, wonder, or laughter, you step into Kairos. And in those moments, you do not grow older; you grow *alive*.

Chronos will continue to tick, but its rhythm no longer defines you. When you master both, you no longer resist time, you ride it. You no longer fear aging, you integrate it. You no longer look back with regret or forward with worry, you stand in the eternal now, fully awake.

To master time is not to escape it. It is to learn its deeper rhythm and become fluent in both its languages: the schedule and the soul. Because in the end, you were never running out of time.

You were only discovering what it means to truly inhabit time. you are not aging. You are unfolding into timelessness.

Conclusion: Embracing the Paradox of Time

As we reach this final reflection, it's clear that time isn't just a simple, linear progression marked by clocks and calendars. Instead, it exists as a dual force - a paradoxical dance between measured moments and those rare, fleeting opportunities that defy measurement. This paradox between Chronos and Kairos challenges our usual ways of navigating life and creativity. Understanding this interplay holds the key to making an impact that echoes far beyond the limits imposed by conventional timekeeping.

The challenge lies in embracing both precision and spontaneity, discipline and intuition, structure and flow. Too often, the modern world insists we prioritize Chronos, the quantifiable ticking of seconds and hours. Deadlines, schedules, and productivity metrics dominate our attention, pulling us into a tunnel vision focused on measurable progress. While this mastery over Chronos is essential for discipline and consistent output, an exclusive commitment to it blinds us to deeper currents of meaning - the Kairos moments when true transformation occurs.

Imagine creativity as a river. Chronos is the steady current, flowing predictably and consistently. Kairos, however, shows up as the unexpected confluences, the whirlpools, the sudden surges of energy that change the river's course. Both are necessary. Without the current, the river stagnates. Without the surges, it remains unremarkable. When we learn to flow with both forces, we open the door to lasting impact - an impact that resonates beyond the technical achievements cataloged by Chronos.

This paradox often creates tension within us. We crave order but long for moments of inspiration. We want to control time, yet we need to surrender to its mysteries. This tension isn't a problem to solve but a dynamic to embrace. Accepting it means recognizing that meaningful contributions - whether in leadership, art, innovation, or personal growth - usually come from balancing measurable effort with intuitive responsiveness.

It's natural to hesitate when faced with uncertainty. Kairos moments don't come with guarantees. Their timing is unpredictable, and their outcomes uncertain. Yet, this unpredictability is the very source of vitality and originality. Those who master time understand that lasting change stems from recognizing and acting within these Kairotic windows. They learn to cultivate awareness, readiness, and the courage to step into opportunity even when it challenges the rigid demands of Chronos.

The paradox of time also urges us to redefine what success means. Instead of only valuing what can be tracked or quantified, we begin to honor the qualitative, subjective experiences that shape our sense of purpose and fulfillment. This shift isn't about abandoning productivity but about enriching it. It's about creating an ecosystem where efficiency serves creativity rather than suppressing it. In this balanced ecosystem, the ticking clock becomes not a tyrant but a partner - guiding us without confining us.

Consider professionals who harness this paradox well. They rigorously manage their schedules, honoring Chronos to maintain momentum and responsibility. Yet, they also remain attuned to Kairos, recognizing when a spontaneous pivot or an off-schedule conversation could unlock innovation or deepen connection. This ability to oscillate fluidly between these modes cultivates resilience and adaptability in a world that rarely unfolds as neatly as planned.

For creatives and lifelong learners, this dance between Chronos and Kairos is especially critical. The pursuit of mastery requires time structured into deliberate practice - hours spent honing skills, absorbing knowledge, and building discipline. But breakthroughs, those instances when insight illuminates the path forward, cannot be rushed or scheduled. They emerge in Kairos moments, often sparked by subtle shifts in awareness or by the willingness to engage with uncertainty without premature conclusions.

This paradox also reveals important truths about how we relate to ourselves and others. When we value both Chronos and Kairos, we cultivate patience without passivity, action without anxiety. We learn to trust the timing of our growth and relationships, to honor both reliability and serendipity. Emotional intelligence flourishes in this space, encouraging deeper empathy and connection because we're no longer enslaved to impatience or rigid expectations.

Our modern dilemma - shaped by technology's pace - both complicates and illuminates this paradox. The constant pulse of digital life magnifies Chronos, fragmenting attention and making it difficult to be fully present when a Kairos moment arises. Yet, technology also offers tools to remind us of our deeper rhythms - to pause, reflect, and realign. Embracing the paradox means wielding technology thoughtfully, using it with intention rather than letting it use us.

Ultimately, embracing the paradox of time leads to a more integrated way of living. It invites us to weave discipline with openness, measurement with meaning, routine with possibility. This integration doesn't just enhance how we work or create. It enriches the very texture of our lives. We begin to perceive time not as a relentless taskmaster but as a collaborator - a mysterious medium through which our deepest intentions find expression.

When we master this integration, the impact we make resonates in both immediate and enduring ways. Actions rooted solely in Chronos may yield results visible today but can feel hollow or unsatisfying over time. Conversely, actions sprung from Kairos connect us to a deeper sense of purpose but may lose grounding if not supported by consistent effort. Bringing these together empowers us to act decisively, creatively, and meaningfully - crafting legacies that endure beyond our lifetimes.

The journey to embrace this paradox is ongoing. It requires patience with ourselves as we move between order and spontaneity, control and surrender. It demands curiosity to explore how time shapes our inner experience and daily choices. And it invites courage to step into moments of uncertainty, trusting that through this tension, true transformation awaits.

In the final reflection, time emerges as more than a resource to manage. It shows itself as the profound context of existence - a rhythm inviting us to grow, create, and connect differently with the world. We become architects not just of moments but of meaningful experiences that ripple through our personal and professional lives.

By embracing this paradox, we stop fighting against the constraints of minutes and deadlines or chasing elusive perfect timing. Instead, we navigate time with grace, harnessing its dual nature to leave a lasting impact - not through sheer quantity of output but through the quality of presence and intention.

In doing so, we don't just survive time. We transform it, becoming active participants in a timeless dance that weaves our stories into the greater tapestry of life.

Appendix: Practical Exercises & Reflection Prompts

Having moved through the rich terrain of time - from the measurable ticks of Chronos to the transformative sparks of Kairos - it's time to bring these insights into active practice. This appendix offers a collection of exercises and reflection prompts designed to deepen your experience and sharpen your understanding of time's multiple dimensions. The invitation here is not simply to learn, but to engage, embody, and ultimately master the way time unfolds in your personal and professional world.

1. Cultivating Awareness of Your Time Experience

Daily Time Mapping

Track your activities in 15-minute intervals for three consecutive days. Pay close attention to how you feel during each segment - rushed or calm, mechanical or inspired. Where does Chronos dominate? When do you sense glimpses of Kairos?

Reflection Prompt

At the end of each day, ask:

Which moments felt alive with opportunity rather than obligation? How did your experience of time shift during these moments?

2. Recognizing and Harnessing Kairos Moments

Opportunity Journaling

Keep a small journal dedicated to Kairos. Each day, note situations where you sensed a meaningful window of opportunity - however subtle or small. Did you act on it, hesitate, or overlook it?

Reflection Prompt

Reflect on one Kairos moment you encountered recently.

What conditions made the moment ripe? How did your mindset influence your ability to seize or miss it?

3. Deepening Relationship with Chronos

Time Discipline Exercise

Select one daily task - such as your morning routine or a focused work session - and perform it with deliberate attention to structure and timing. Set a start and end time and focus only on that task within the boundary.

Reflection Prompt

Afterward, ask yourself:

How did intentional boundaries affect your focus and energy? Did working with Chronos improve efficiency or surface new insights?

4. Balancing Chronos and Kairos in Decision Making

Decision Window Practice

When facing a choice, pause to identify what elements are Chronos-driven (deadlines, scheduling, efficiency) and what elements feel Kairos-driven (intuition, emotional readiness, deeper alignment). Write down each influence before deciding.

Reflection Prompt

How did noticing these two temporal forces shape your decision? Did Kairos play a role in the outcome or shift your level of clarity and confidence?

5. Creating a Personal Time Mastery Framework

Values and Time Alignment

List your top core values. Then review how your current time investments reflect (or disconnect from) those values. Where is Chronos pulling you into misalignment? Where is Kairos inviting deeper connection?

Reflection Prompt

What adjustments could bring more harmony between how you spend time and what matters most? How can you design your days to intentionally blend Chronos structure with Kairos rhythm in service of your highest intentions?

6. Embracing the Flow of Time Through Mindfulness

Mindful Time Check-In

Set a soft alarm three times per day. When it sounds, pause and ask yourself:

Am I experiencing time as pressure, presence, or possibility right now?

Reflection Prompt

At the end of the week, reflect on the overall effect:

Did moments of presence increase? How did these pauses influence your creativity, relationships, or calm?

These exercises are more than daily practices - they are invitations to step fully into the lived experience of time. They call for curiosity, honesty, and the willingness to explore how time, in all its forms, quietly shapes your choices, emotions, and growth.

By engaging regularly, you strengthen a relationship not just with the outer mechanics of the clock, but with the inner rhythms that guide purpose, timing, and presence. Time mastery is not about controlling every minute. It is about moving with awareness, adapting with clarity, and cultivating the readiness to meet each moment - measured or meaningful - with your full attention.

In this way, time becomes not a race to finish, but a path to walk with presence and intention. Not something to fight or fear, but something to collaborate with - a resource and rhythm that, when honored, can lead you closer to the life you are meant to create.

www.ingramcontent.com/pod-product-compliance
Lightning Source LLC
Chambersburg PA
CBHW051951290426
44110CB00015B/2201